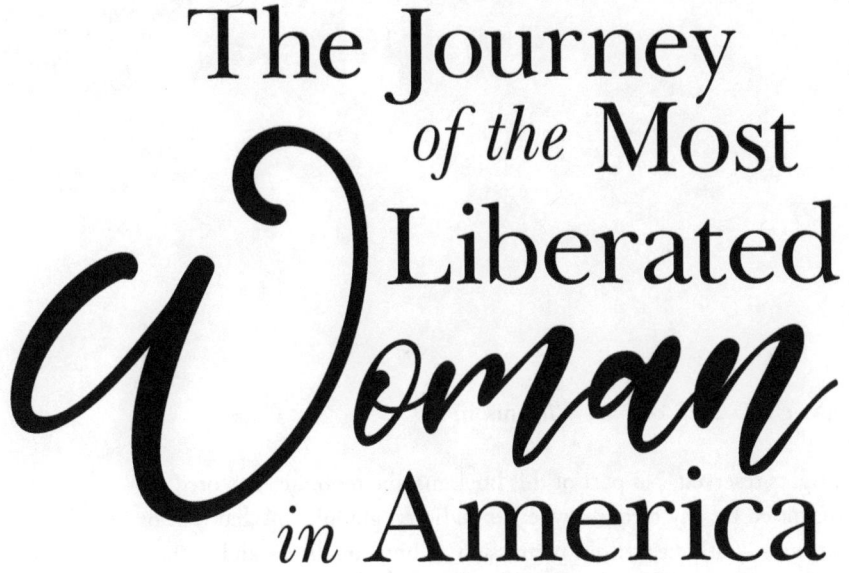

The Journey of the Most Liberated Woman in America

Barbara Williamson

Copyright © 2022 Barbara Williamson.

All rights reserved. No part of this book may be reproduced, stored, or transmitted by any means—whether auditory, graphic, mechanical, or electronic—without written permission of both publisher and author, except in the case of brief excerpts used in critical articles and reviews. Unauthorized reproduction of any part of this work is illegal and is punishable by law.

ISBN: 979-8-88640-256-8 (sc)
ISBN: 979-8-88640-257-5 (hc)
ISBN: 979-8-88640-258-2 (e)

Because of the dynamic nature of the Internet, any web addresses or links contained in this book may have changed since publication and may no longer be valid. The views expressed in this work are solely those of the author and do not necessarily reflect the views of the publisher, and the publisher hereby disclaims any responsibility for them.

One Galleria Blvd., Suite 1900, Metairie, LA 70001
1-888-421-2397

ALWAYS IN OUR THOUGHTS

John Williamson was a man who could not be described; he had to be experienced. He never met a problem too big or complex to solve. For those not lucky enough to meet him, he was something like that famous quote from Theodore Roosevelt: "Speak softly and carry a big stick." Only his big stick was never violence but rather cogency. His ideas were always perceptive, spot-on, and carried great weight that belied his folksy, calm appearance. Yet his sharp wit that punctured so many foolish ideas was never turned against people.

His ideas were before their time. Perhaps his ideas were before all times, for he dared to take off his mask and show his true face. This is something few men choose to do. What was most unique about John was not necessarily the wonderful person he was but rather the way he accepted and embraced life with a candor that takes great courage. He urged us all to take off the masks we wear and make the world a more honest place … the sort of honesty that inspires trust that inspires appreciation and love.

—John Burkitt

He always held himself to the highest standards. Honest and always true to his word, he showed the world his brand of loving kindness. A shining example of what it means to be tender, trustworthy, loving, compassionate, and caring, he was always mindful not to cause pain.

John, my beloved partner of forty-seven years, your love sustained me to grow into a real human being. Your memories live on forever in my heart.

—Barbara

PREFACE

The Journey of the Most Liberated Woman in America is a joyous romp through the sexual revolution of the sixties. My life partner, John, and I created the first (and perhaps the only) commune for grown-ups where open sexuality was encouraged and fully embraced. We called it Sandstone Retreat. Nestled in the wooded splendor of Topanga Canyon, California, with sweeping vistas of the Malibu Mountains and Pacific Ocean, it was fifteen acres of beauty and pleasure, a retreat from artificiality. It was a community where a person's mind, body, and sexuality came together in total abandonment. The dress code was total nudity, and the mind-set was acceptance of all things pleasurable, sensual, and sexual. Sandstone was a huge success from the moment we opened our doors, and dozens of celebrities came to stay and play. I can honestly say I saw more naked stars than any other woman of that era! We offered such a unique and tantalizing lifestyle that soon reporters and television producers were clamoring for us to go public about our amazing concept of shared sexual pleasure without jealousy or possessiveness. Gay Talese's wildly successful best seller *Thy Neighbor's Wife* was about life at Sandstone. Articles written about Sandstone are too numerous to list, but just a few highlights include *Esquire* (three times), *Rolling Stone*, the *Los Angeles Times*, *Atlantic Monthly*, *Time Magazine*, *Penthouse*, and the *Los Angeles Star*. We were also prominently featured in television specials that aired on the History Channel, VH1, Lifetime, and the Sundance Channel.

Presiding over all that free love and open sexuality was an experience of a lifetime. I came to recognize and embrace my own bisexual nature and to share it with others. When I look back on those years spent at Sandstone, I appreciate how truly wondrous it was, how amazing and unique, and John and I were the creators.

When it finally came to an end, as all things must, we spent the next few years traveling. We settled in Fallon, Nevada. It soon came to our attention that several abandoned tigers were facing euthanasia, and John sprang into action. We have ten acres of land, and with the help of some wonderful volunteers, we built a compound and rescued them. That was the birth of Tiger Touch, a haven for any and all big cats to live out their lives in peace and love. We've taken in numerous big cats over the years—lions, tigers, lynx, servals, cougars—whoever needed a home.

As I sit here at my computer, Peggy Sue, the love of my life, a very large lynx, is sprawled in the chair next to me. She lives in the house with us and follows me around like a gentle puppy. So I guess you could say I'm still sharing the love!

ACKNOWLEDGEMENTS

From Barbara Williamson

To my special friend Nancy Bacon, I am so grateful for you and your extraordinary organizational talent, profound insights, and exceptional writing skills, which have all made this book a reality.

A special thank you to all Sandstone members (too numerous to mention here) who stood behind us with such great courage, trust, and belief while we endeavored to create and improve relationships between men and women.

To Say Thank You
For Buying A Copy Of This Book

Exclusive Interview Bundle with Barbara Williamson

I am offering you an exclusive audio bundle in which I shared my controversial Sandstone Retreat in Malibu, California in the early '60s and '70's

Visit barbarawilliamson.com
to know more about the era of the free love and the sexual revolution.

Chapter 1

SANDSTONE WAS MY HAVEN. A safe, wondrous, and joyful retreat from artificiality situated high in the magnificent, wildly beautiful, wooded tangle of Topanga Canyon just north of Los Angeles, it nestled on the crest of a mountain like a gentle Buddha. A lovely rambling mission-style mansion overlooked the chaparral-covered Malibu mountain range. The panoramic view swept down over Santa Monica Bay to the island of Catalina. High above the smog of the city, the air was crisp and clean with the tangy scent of pine and the perfume of wildflowers that dotted the rugged terrain. This lush yet rugged fifteen- acre estate with its perfectly manicured, terraced lawns was my home. I was in the main house on that warm late afternoon sitting on a plush velvet sofa at one end of the sixty-foot-long living room. And I was, of course, naked. I say of course because the dozen or more people with me were naked as well.

My home was often called Sandstone Retreat or, more formally, Sandstone Foundation for Community Systems Research, a place for living in open sexual freedom and seeking to eliminate sexual possessiveness and jealousy. Founded by my life partner, John Williamson, and I, Sandstone was a family of like-minded people who came together with one goal in mind: to be themselves. They all wished to shed their everyday lives and retreat from the noise and smog of the city; the traffic; and the uptight, puritanical conventions that attempted to keep us obedient to the mores of the day—females in their neat little skirts and blouses and sensible shoes, males in their obligatory suits and ties. These rules did not exist at Sandstone.

In fact, there were no rules at Sandstone. We simply asked that everyone there do no harm to any living thing. Any show of affection, kindness, friendship, or sexuality is a good thing. We offered a sensual playground for adults, a haven where all senses were explored and enjoyed.

As I relaxed against the deep velvet cushions of the sofa on that lazy day, I was filled with profound pleasure. I felt velvet on my bare skin. The softly flickering lights of strobes and candles cast shadows on the nude bodies of my housemates, softening them. One end of the plush, carpeted living room was dominated by a gigantic stone fireplace. Several of my nude friends lay on the floor, their bodies shadowed by the dancing flames. Occasionally, someone would reach out and lightly stroke the bare hip of the person next to him or her, and lips would touch and linger a moment. It didn't matter whose hip or whose lips, as long as it was a pleasurable experience for both parties. Open sexuality was embraced at Sandstone. Our roster of friends, guests, and members over the years was impressive by anyone's standards. It seemed everyone—the famous and the not so famous—found their way up the narrow, treacherous, winding road that led to Sandstone. Bobby Darin, Peter Lawford, Timothy Leary, Daniel Ellsberg (of Pentagon Papers fame), *Paris Review* editor George Plimpton, Dean Martin, Sammy Davis Jr.—the list is endless.

Sandstone Main House - Front view with pond

Sandstone Main House - Ocean view

I remember the night Sammy Davis Jr. showed up with his wife, Altovise, and their friend, the porn star Marilyn Chambers. She was starring in the hit movie *Behind the Green Door*. She had replaced Linda Lovelace (of *Deep Throat* fame) as the reigning queen of porn. Marty Zitter, a fast-talking, exuberant, amiable, tanned, fit, and stark-naked host, met them at the door. They were met as all guests were—with a big bear hug.

Sammy laughed uproariously, clapped his hands together as he looked around at all the nude bodies lounging on furniture and floor, and said, "Wow! This is one warm cat! I think I could really get into this place!" He promptly shrugged out of his Nehru jacket and let it drop to the thick carpet. He tossed his cuff links (at least ten carats worth of diamonds) on top. Marilyn scrambled across the floor on her hands and knees to quickly scoop them up and drop them down her cleavage!

Everyone in the room laughed. Sammy casually lit a cigarette with a diamond-encrusted lighter and tossed the lighter to Marilyn. He took Altovise by the hand and led her downstairs to the ballroom, doing a soft-shoe on the way. The ballroom existed for one purpose: sexual pleasure. The slowly rotating mirror ball hanging from the ceiling speckled the writhing, naked bodies with flecks of pastel colors as they copulated on the wall-to-wall mattresses. In the sixties and seventies, intercourse was often referred to as "balling"—hence the ballroom. It also brought to mind days of yore, a beautifully appointed room where couples danced cheek to cheek and groin to groin, experiencing a mutual eroticism. And yes, there was a changing of partners. It was perfectly acceptable for someone to cut in and finish the dance with a different partner. At Sandstone, we just did it horizontally rather than vertically! Actually, though, I do remember a lot of vertical couplings in our huge indoor swimming pool.

What a magnificent Olympic-sized pool it was. It was underneath a towering beamed ceiling and surrounded in rustic splendor with lush foliage, tall trees, large rocks, and the sweet perfume of flowering bushes. We brought the outside inside. We kept the water at 93 degrees, very close to body temperature. I often felt like it was a returning to the womb, a warm embrace, secure yet with total freedom of weightlessness, floating in the embryo sac. What a delicious feeling!

John was an aerospace engineer turned free-love visionary. I was a top national salesperson for a major insurance company. We carved out a utopian commune in these wild chaparral-covered hills, and together we embarked on a radical social experiment. We would live in total sexual freedom, where sexual possessiveness and jealousy did not exist. We wanted a new kind of community, a place where a person's mind, body, and being were no longer strangers to each other. At Sandstone we could instill a feeling of relaxed freedom and embrace the idea that the body is good, that open expressions of affection and sexuality are good, that a person may do anything he or she wants—as long as it's not offensive to anyone else. The only rule at Sandstone was to do no harm—not to try to force your desires on others. If they accepted you, fine. If they didn't, also fine. If Sandstone had a motto, it would have been from the old Frederick S. Perls poem: "I do my thing, and you do your thing. I am not in this world to live up to your expectations and you are not in this world to live up to mine. You are you and I am I and if by chance we find each other, it's beautiful."

There were no structured activities at Sandstone, no programs of behavioral study, no sitting in a circle discussing our innermost fears and personal hang-ups, no basket-weaving classes or lessons in macramé or pottery. Our unity lay in a deep-seated need for honesty, sharing, and freedom from all things artificial. There was no shallow cocktail-party banter. No one hid behind expensive clothing and jewelry or high-paying careers.

Music genius Berry Gordy showed up one night dressed to the nines in a gold Armani suit, two-inch-high patent leather platform boots, and designer shades, with multiple gold chains around his neck, a large diamond earring, and rings on every finger. I invited him to get nude, relax, and mingle with the others. "Oh no," he replied, shocked. "If I take off my clothes, no one will know who I am!"

At Sandstone, the point was the complete opposite. Once you took off your clothes and got real, everyone knew who you were and loved you for it. You were no longer hiding behind a layer of expensive clothing that showed the world how wealthy and hip you were. No low-slung, hip-riding bell bottoms and tie-dyed T-shirts proclaimed your disdain of the establishment. No military or law-enforcement uniforms declared your allegiance. No thousand- dollar Armani suits or five-hundred-dollar calfskin attaché cases advertised your status as a high-powered banker or attorney. When you shed your public persona and stand naked with a group of other naked people, incredible lightness washes over you. All pretense and game-playing are gone.

After spending most of the afternoon relaxing against the soft velvet cushions of the sofa, visiting with friends, and sharing a joint and a glass of wine, I stood and raised my arms above my head, stretching like a contented cat. Several people milled about the living room, chatting, having a snack, exchanging ideas, ridding themselves of the tensions of their daily routines in the "real world" of the city and unwinding in the serenity of Sandstone. I drifted downstairs to the ballroom to see how things were going. Shadows from the mirror ball softly highlighted the naked, writhing bodies of a dozen or more couples. Touching and stimulating beautiful, well-rounded breasts to erect nipples, seeking fingers, undulating buttocks, backs glistening with sweat, wet lips murmuring soft words of encouragement, open mouths in the ecstasy of orgasm: all was as it should be. An aura of peaceful sensuality prevailed.

As my eyes adjusted to the dim lighting, I was suddenly jolted by the stillness of a lone figure lying on his side, his eyes seemingly unseeing as he stared into the shadows. His six-foot-plus body was nude and rock hard, each muscle clearly defined by taut white skin unrelieved in its starkness by any substantial amount of body hair. One huge fist was propped under his chin. His teeth were clenched, and I saw his jaw muscles bunch spasmodically. His erect penis lay across his inner thigh. Nothing moved. Nothing twitched. He was obviously caught up in some terrible animallike conflict, teetering on the edge of a primitive decision. I remembered that he was a veteran police officer skilled in the ways of cold violence, lean and mean. I remembered the swagger in his walk, his casual use of the word *nigger,* and his scorn for "long-haired, hippie pricks," whom he bragged about harassing every chance he got. He lived and worked in a fashionable, upscale suburb of San Diego and was quite proud of keeping it safe for the waspish residents. I felt a shiver slide down my spine as I looked into the dull flatness of his eyes. The pupils were dilated, and his lips were drawn back from his teeth in a feral snarl.

I followed his gaze and saw his wife sprawled a few feet away. She was a beautiful woman, tall and lushly curved with dreamy eyes. She glistened with sweat, her pale arms and legs wrapped securely around the two hundred pounds of black maleness that held her close. He suddenly raised himself above her, balancing on stiff arms as he plunged his rock-hard black penis deep inside.

I heard a guttural whimper escape from the cop's drawn lips, and I moved forward to lay a soothing hand on his arm. He flinched and turned tortured eyes toward me. I smiled and leaned against him, comforting him with soft murmurs and a gentle touch. At that moment the black man and the cop's wife reached simultaneous orgasm in a screaming crescendo of ecstasy. I lifted my head from his shoulder and looked up into his face. Tears were streaming down his cheeks. His penis was flaccid.

As if just noticing my presence beside him, he turned and gave me the sweetest smile, his eyes soft and shiny with tears, and he gathered me close in strong, warm arms. On the adjoining mattress his wife and her black lover were still intertwined and sighing softly in the last throes of their climax. Her eyes were closed; then she suddenly opened them and sought out her husband's face. Her full lips were swollen with passion, her dark hair wildly tumbled about her bare shoulders, her white breasts still crushed against his ebony chest. There was a heartbeat of stillness. Then this dangerous racist, this chauvinistic, tough-as-nails lawman lurched forward and gathered his wife and her black lover into his wide embrace. His large hands cupped the backs of their heads, bringing them to rest on his shoulders, and the lovers' arms encircled him, drawing him closer. They stayed that way for several minutes, plaited together like black and white braids, gently rocking one another. They exuded a sense of profound peace like a heavenly aura. Remember, this was the late sixties, when African Americans were still vilified by white America. In many states blacks were not even allowed to sit at the same lunch counter with whites, so having sex was truly an amazing breakthrough, an affirmation that love conquers all.

We called it the Sandstone experience.

Chapter 2

I WALKED SLOWLY UPSTAIRS TO THE living room. It had grown dark, and I could see through the sliding glass door outside to the balcony where a shadowed figure sat on a chair, his feet propped upon the railing. The tip of his cigarette glowed in the dark. His head was tilted back, and he was gazing up at the star-filled sky. Cicadas, crickets, and night frogs joined together in a euphony of song, and I could just barely hear the muted spill of a waterfall in the far distance.

I lay my hand on his shoulder, and he reached up to cover it with his much larger one, gently tugging me down to sit in the chair next to him. Our fingers intertwined, and he playfully swung our hands back and forth. The night air was soft and warm, gently caressing our nude bodies as John and I sat in companionable silence. Deep, satisfying love flowed between us without a word being spoken. We were the true definition of soul mates. How had I gotten so lucky, I wondered, when my humble beginning of life had been so sad and painful?

I was born Barbara Cramer on April 5, 1939, on a midsized farm near Chamois, Missouri, where I grew up alone and unwanted. To this day I cannot remember ever feeling any love from either of my parents. There was never any hugging or touching or kisses. I'm sure I wasn't even rocked as a baby. My earliest memories are of misery and solitude.

The farm was isolated, and we had no close neighbors; therefore I had no children to play with. I never thought of my house as a home. It was just a silent, cold building where I slept. When I lay in bed at night, my brain churned with questions: *Who am I? Why am I here? Why doesn't anyone talk to me, touch me, or love me? Why am I so unlovable and alone?*

I couldn't bear being in that cold building, so I spent every spare moment in the woods. There were inviting sounds in the woods, ever so soothing sounds. The singing of the birds, the chattering of squirrels and chipmunks, the yip of coyotes and red fox, the splash of trout leaping from the creek, the soft churring of raccoons and possums. These sounds were a welcome song to a lonely child.

The minute I got home from school, I grabbed my fishing pole and a can of worms I had dug from the damp earth and headed for the nearby creek. With my dog, Boots, leading the way, we ran through waist-high grass and weeds to settle ourselves on the bank of the stream. The water, too, was musical, splashing and gurgling over rocks and fallen logs. I would cast my line into the water and watch the cork bounce and bob, waiting for a fish to take the bait and pull it under. I didn't really care if I caught a fish or not. I just loved visiting with my forest friends and listening to their songs.

Sixteen years of spending the majority of my time in the woods gave me a deep and abiding love of nature. The natural beauty overwhelmed my senses. I loved the towering majestic trees and lush thickness of wild lavender bushes and alfalfa shrubs; the spongy softness of pine needles and moss muted my steps as I meandered through sun-dappled meadows.

Those years I spent in the woods communicating with nature and all the little furry critters saved my life. I was completely accepted by them. They showed no fear, only a natural curiosity. *If these wild creatures like me*, I thought, *perhaps I'm not so unlovable after all. Maybe someday someone else will love me.*

But it sure as hell wasn't going to be my father! The day after I graduated from high school, he said (and I quote verbatim), "Okay, I've supported you long enough. It's time for you to get out and support yourself."

Apparently he had chosen to forget that I had supported myself—that is, as much as any twelve-year-old can. I worked every summer during school break and earned enough to buy whatever personal items I needed. I certainly didn't get any little extras from my parents—just the obligatory bed and board.

From as early as I can remember, my main goal in life was to get the hell away! I didn't care where—just away! Away from the coldness and lack of love, away from narrow-minded ignorance. I had seen (and loved) the movie *Auntie Mame* and had decided that was the lifestyle I wanted. I yearned to be around brilliant, cultured, interesting people, to exchange ideas and grow and learn. I wasn't eager to get married, have children, and join the PTA. I wanted to live and enjoy life. I wanted to earn good money and have nice clothes and a new car. I had very little respect for men. I saw them as selfish, aggressive, narcissistic, arrogant, and unfeeling. Why in the world would I want a dolt like that hanging around and contaminating my environment? No thanks. I would make it on my own.

I did have one good friend from school, Frances, and she shared my vision, so it took very little convincing to get her to move with me to Kansas City, Missouri. We stayed with my aunt and uncle and began looking for jobs. This proved next to impossible for two teenagers just out of high school, so we moved on to St. Louis and had better luck in a bigger city. The jobs didn't amount to much, but they paid us enough to rent a cute little apartment, buy new clothes, and start learning how to live as adults.

I've always hated cold weather, and the winters in St. Louis were brutal. Luckily, Frances felt the same way. We both hated bulky winter clothing and snow boots, so one day one of us (I can't remember who) said, "You know, we should move to Hollywood. We can just lie around under palm trees, eat fresh oranges, and date movie stars!"

"And no more thick sweaters and itchy wool pants! We'll live in shorts and sandals and cute little summer dresses!"

"And bikinis!" We collapsed together in giggles, filled with the optimism and bravado of youth. Within the week we had packed up and headed west. Serendipitously, Frances had an aunt living in upscale Los Angeles, and she was delighted to have us stay with her as long as we wanted. It was a fairytale come true.

It didn't take long for both of us to find jobs, buy a used car, and start learning how to make our way through the numerous scary freeways intersecting that sprawling city. We only stayed with Aunt Effie for about three months before we had enough money to rent our own apartment in Hollywood. We were so anxious to be on our own, to be grown-ups at last!

Our apartment had a beautiful pool, so of course we rushed out and bought our first bikinis. I had always had a nice body—curves in all the right places, nice full breasts, good legs, not an ounce of extra fat. We hung out at the pool a lot and met other young people who invited us to parties and helped us navigate those early months in our new world. Southern California was everything I dreamed it would be: warm, sunny, and filled with palm trees, convertibles, orange groves, swimming pools, and movie studios. Everyone sported a dark, healthy tan and wore as little clothing as possible. There was a feeling of lush sensuality in the air, a softness that gently caressed my skin. Even the rain was soft and warm—not like the slanting hard, icy needles of St. Louis. Now that my home life was happy and secure, I turned my attention to finding a career that would afford me the best opportunity to grow. And earn big bucks!

Insurance probably seems like a dull choice, but I knew it would offer me the chance to develop my sales and people skills. Also, there was no discrimination against women in the insurance business. Male or female, you were as good as your sales. Within just a few short months I was managing the insurance departments of four automobile dealerships. I worked about four or five hours a day (leaving me plenty of time to play!), and I was earning a very prestigious income.

By age twenty-two I was earning a high five-figure income—this in the early sixties when most women were five-dollar-an-hour secretaries or "just housewives." I bought a brand-new Ford convertible with a canary-yellow bottom and bold black top. And wow, the sun sure felt great on my face as I zoomed around Hollywood with the top down!

John's voice pulled me back through time. "Ready to go back inside, pumpkin?" I smiled at the nickname. For some silly reason he always called me pumpkin. A gentle but chilly breeze had begun to sweep through Topanga Canyon, sending goose bumps and shivers across our naked flesh. It was late summer, really hot during the day but quickly cooling off in the evening in readiness for autumn.

Still holding hands, we went inside and stood for a moment in the living room. Several housemates were scattered around the gigantic room, talking, having a cocktail or glass of wine, sharing a joint, or simply gazing at the dancing flames in the fireplace. A feeling of pleasure and camaraderie enveloped the room like a warm and fuzzy blanket.

Sandstone Living Room

As I gazed around, I was filled with satisfied pride, because I had decorated this room with one thought in mind: everything must feel good to the skin. Couches and chairs were upholstered in soft, sensual velvet. There were no leather sofas for skin to stick to and no scratchy wool or stiff brocades or gaudy synthetic fabrics. The shag carpet was deep and plush. Pastel lights and strobes overhead cast everything below in a sort of mystical, magical glow. The living room flowed into the dining room, and beyond that was a bar with a regulation-sized pool table. There were three bedrooms inside for those of us who lived at Sandstone year round, and outside several cottages were available for more guests. The kitchen was well appointed, warm, and welcoming.

As I looked around I realized how many times the words *warm, soft,* and *sensual* came to mind. Those words, or course, were the direct opposite of the words I associated with my childhood experience—*cold, harsh,* and *unyielding.* I had been so psychologically damaged by my loveless childhood that I had sought to erase it completely from my mind by surrounding myself in all things that felt good.

I think that's probably why I enjoy making love with women. They are soft and satin smooth, whereas men are hard and hairy! I think maybe I also had an unrealistic desire to return to the womb where it was warm and safe. I've often wondered if parents realize how much irrevocable damage they do to children when they don't show them love. As an adult I gave and received love freely—and I never wanted to have children. I saw no reason to further populate an already overpopulated world. Therefore, it was rather odd that I became known as "Earth Mother" to all the guests and members of Sandstone. And odder still that I enjoyed the title!

Very early in life I began questioning my own sexuality. I was a tomboy, so did this mean I was a lesbian? I enjoyed sex with men but didn't realize it wasn't quite enough until I had my first sexual experience with a woman. I had never heard the word *bisexual* until I was in my twenties, but it fit me perfectly. I just didn't know it then. I was so curious about sexuality—everyone's sexuality—it began to consume my thoughts. I didn't want to believe sex was bad and dirty. (It felt too good!) And I sure as hell didn't believe it was for procreation. The world was already filled to overflowing with countless unwanted, abandoned babies. If people were having sex just to produce babies, then why did they abandon them, abort them, give them up for adoption? I decided that sex must have been invented simply for play and pleasure. Our bodies are built so all parts fit together for just one reason: to stimulate and satisfy all the other parts.

I decided very early on that I did not want the conventional relationship—marriage, children, fidelity—but it never occurred to me that I would meet a man who felt the exact same way. But I'm getting ahead of myself. First there was a sort of testing-the-water period when I dated and experimented with my sexuality. I was attracted to women, but same-sex relationships were still frowned upon even though the sexual revolution was knocking at the door of the still-young decade of the sixties. It was the Age of Aquarius, the rise of women's lib, civil rights, the Vietnam War, a time that saw the assassination of our young president, a time of turmoil and change. Marijuana replaced martinis. Timothy Leary encouraged us to "turn on, tune, in and drop out," so I began experimenting with psychedelic drugs—mescaline, LSD, magic mushrooms. They expanded my brain and allowed me to journey off the normal path of acceptable sex.

In 1964 I joined the New York Life Insurance Company and began a career in sales that proved to be very lucrative. Within a year I ranked in the top one hundred of the company's sales force and achieved the number one national sales position in health insurance. I joined the Los Angeles Toastmistresses Club and won an award for giving the best talk. I gave motivational speeches at other New York Life sales offices and wrote articles encouraging other women to enter the field of insurance. In short, I had achieved the financial goals that the women's liberation movement and the Equal Opportunity Act would later come to support. I thoroughly enjoyed the independence that came with enough money to pay my own way. I dined in the finest restaurants, drove a brand-new car, owned closets full of designer clothes, and was blissfully single and free. I was a success.

With my financial security and the praise of my colleagues I developed a very healthy self-confidence. Word was out: Don't fuck with Barbara Cramer! My self-respect was so obvious a lot of guys simply steered clear of me, realizing their line of bullshit wouldn't work with me. But of course there were still a lot of guys who thought they were superior both intellectually and sexually. After all, I was just a girl—albeit a very pretty one with brains and a great body. I was cute rather than beautiful, with an elfin appeal that would often be compared to Meg Ryan. I guess it was the combination of innocent face and sexy body that guys found so appealing, because I was constantly being hit on. And always by the same type of vain, swaggering, macho, chauvinistic Neanderthal who gloried in their own misguided belief that males ruled and females drooled. Yuck!

If that was all I had to choose from for a life partner, I preferred to be alone. That was kind of difficult in a world where the old Cinderella myth was still very much alive. The handsome prince would suddenly appear out of nowhere astride his white steed and sweep the helpless damsel away to live happily ever after in his magnificent castle. The fairytales never mentioned the castle was surrounded by a dark and ominous moat that kept the princess a virtual prisoner. And if that wasn't confining enough, the poor girl was also strapped into a chastity belt to keep her untouched while the good prince battled in some far-off crusade. Apparently it wasn't enough that the belt prevented anyone else from touching her; she couldn't even touch herself! No playful masturbation to while away the time waiting for her prince to return. Ah, the cruel injustice of it all!

But that's the bullshit men have been forcing on women down through the ages: Me Tarzan, you Jane. I'll marry you and pay the bills, and all you have to do is support me in all things; cook; clean; decorate; have children (and become a taxi driver for said children until the age of maturity); be ready for sex whenever I want it (and always praise my sexual prowess, telling me what a huge penis I have); take care of me and baby me when I'm sick; stroke my ego; don't talk when I'm watching sports on TV; always be well groomed; and always tell your family and friends how wonderful I am and how lucky you are. And guess what, baby? I'll give you my name!

Well, I ask you, what silly little girl's head wouldn't be turned by an offer like that? *Mine.* I was not, nor had I ever been, a silly little girl, and I was much too smart to settle. There was someone out there, someone with vision, a man with loftier goals and a kindred spirit. I just had to find him. I was only twenty-six and in no hurry.

Chapter 3

TO THIS DAY I STILL don't fully understand why I made the decision to throw away an extremely successful and very lucrative career and plunge headfirst into the unknown arena of sexual exploration. Sure, it was the swinging sixties, and the sexual revolution had exploded like millions of fireworks going off all at once, but most people were simply enjoying the falling sparks. I was prepared to give it all up. The lifestyle I had worked like a dog to obtain in the past decade didn't seem that important anymore. The exploding fireworks of the sixties, the climate of political unrest, and the revolutionary changes that were sweeping the nation set off a tiny spark of rebellion that still lived deep inside me. I had conformed to the mores of the day and put in my time behind a desk. I had dressed appropriately in neat little business suits, trim pumps, and short, unpolished nails. I had even, at times, strapped my breasts down beneath my blouses so my male colleagues wouldn't be distracted by their size and label me sexy—i.e., not serious enough to compete in the business world.

Well, I not only competed, I excelled! At just twenty-six years old, I was on top the world I had chosen for myself. Why, then, did this little glimmer of light still exist deep inside my subconscious? I recognized it as a challenge to my basic risk-taking, adventurous nature. When I was a child, I would sit in that quiet forest, still as a statue, and wait for the wary approach of a wild bobcat or coyote. I knew their natural curiosity would bring them close enough to check me out as a potential danger. The thrill (and success) for me came when the animals sat quietly instead of running away in fear. I knew I meant them no harm. The satisfaction came from watching them realize it—and accept my presence in their habitat.

That was quite an accomplishment for a little kid. Most adults aren't that brave. But I wasn't just testing my bravery. I was scared, of course. What intelligent person wouldn't be afraid of a wild, unpredictable animal? I simply wanted to know if I would be accepted.

I admit I was a little frightened of that challenging spark in the pit of my belly. It was just a glimpse of an unknown vision but one I knew I had to follow.

The day of my conversion began like any other day. I punched off my alarm at seven o'clock, rolled out of bed, and put on the coffee pot. I even remember what I wore that day—a blue and white seersucker suit. I had flattened my breasts as I always did when I had an important business meeting. My natural brown hair was tucked under a short blond wig. For some odd reason, I thought it gave me a more mature, professional look. Grabbing my purse and portfolio, I hurried to the garage and slid behind the wheel of my brand-new bright red Mustang convertible. My appointment was in Chatsworth, so I eased onto the westbound Ventura Freeway and zipped along with the early-morning traffic. The top was down, and a light breeze ruffled my hair. The sun felt great on my face. I was happy and filled with excitement about my appointment with a prospective client who was interested in a group health policy for his electronics firm. Corporate accounts always got my blood rushing, because they often led to tremendous amounts of new business.

Within seconds of giving my name to the receptionist, John Williamson came into the lobby and personally escorted me into his office. Once inside I stood in shocked silence for a moment, staring at the huge, stark painting of a raging yellow desert that hung behind his desk. The painting was split down the middle by a straight black road that forked suddenly and then disappeared on either side of bright red mountains and a vivid, piercing blue sky. Only a small black rock and a dismal gray cactus relieved the isolation of the scene. I admit to being a little shaken by the ugly yet compelling painting as I sat in the only chair available directly across from the painting and John's messy desk. The desk was piled high with a jumbled array of papers and a large ashtray overflowing with cigarette butts. This certainly didn't look like the office of a corporate vice president!

There were no other paintings on the walls, no stuffed fish or trophies, no diplomas of excellence, no photographs with celebrities or politicians. There wasn't room on his piled-high, messy desk to display a photo of wife and kiddies. A sudden moment of panic gripped me, and my mind went blank. Oh my God, I had forgotten what I had come for! Nervously, I pointed and blurted out, "What does that painting mean to you?"

He gave a charming shrug. "Nothing, I just painted it to shock people into realizing they have to make their own decisions without an advance guarantee of the outcome."

Huh? "Oh, well, yes …" I couldn't remember one word of my usual sales pitch, so I plunged into my portfolio and pulled out my data on the company's employees. I immediately felt more confident with a handful of papers and quickly scanned the contents. John Williamson was married but separated. I looked him over. Plain features, blue eyes, blond hair, average height, quite overweight, nothing special. But there was something—something mysterious, an aura that seemed to draw me closer. He was soft- spoken and gentle.

I was absolutely baffled by my nervousness. I didn't know what had come over me. I quickly began explaining the generalities of a group plan, and he sat quietly listening. Then he gave me a sweet smile and said he wasn't ready to make a decision.

I don't remember leaving his office. I'm sure it was a hasty retreat. By the time I stepped into the elevator leading to my office I felt completely disoriented. I couldn't disengage myself from the sense of immersion I had felt in the presence of John Williamson. Three weeks passed with no word, and still that meeting haunted me like a physical being. What the hell. I picked up the phone and called, inviting John to lunch to discuss the group policy.

The soft, honeyed voice slid through the phone. "I can't make it today, but I'll be glad to take you to dinner tomorrow night."

In my best, crisp business voice, I responded, "Fine. We'll discuss the insurance policy."

"Of course. Seven okay?"

He was prompt, and I was ready. I wore a simple black cocktail dress and a double strand of pearls. I did not flatten my breasts. Even though this was the era of women's lib and I had been opening my own car door for years, I still felt a wave of femininity pass over me as he opened the door of his gold Grand Prix and gallantly helped me inside. It reminded me of those silly Rock Hudson and Doris Day movies, and I had an unfamiliar urge to giggle.

We went to the Hollywood Hills Hotel restaurant and sat outside on the balcony overlooking the neon brilliance of the city below. I was thoroughly intrigued by this unassuming, soft-spoken man. After dinner we went into the cocktail lounge and continued to talk until after one in the morning. I found myself opening up and telling him exactly how I felt about life. I had no intention of ever getting married, having children, or depending on a man. I could take care of myself, thank you very much. John just smiled and said, "Hey, let's go to San Francisco."

Don't ask me why I said yes, but I did, and at 3:00 a.m. we were standing in line at Los Angeles International Airport buying tickets for San Francisco! So far this man had surprised me at every turn, and he surprised me again as we stood at the registration desk in the luxurious

San Francisco Hilton—and John asked for separate rooms! The desk clerk looked as surprised as I felt.

Okay, I told myself as we were being escorted to our rooms, *I see what's happening. John wants to be in control. He obviously wants to approach our relationship cautiously, become friends before lovers.* If indeed were to become lovers. This guy had me off balance, and I wasn't used to that. I was the one who had always been in control and called the shots, but suddenly I found myself perfectly content to let him take the lead. Will wonders never cease!

The next morning I called a couple of girlfriends who were living in the city and invited them over for coffee and catching up. John called and invited us to his suite for a champagne brunch, which quickly turned into a round table discussion of our sex lives. Once again I was surprised by this rather nondescript man. He was totally at ease in the company of women. There was nothing showy or aggressive about him—just a simple, genuine warmth and charm that had all of us hanging on his every word. At one point, one of my girlfriends whispered, "I think the guy's crazy about you!"

I gave a nervous little laugh and said, "No way. I just met the dude!" But I sure as hell was feeling something. The sexual tension between us was obvious, at least on my side. I still wasn't sure how John felt.

That afternoon we toured the city, taking in the sights and sounds of Chinatown, the Settlement, the Wharf, and other odd, little-known underground clubs and transvestite bars. John definitely had a taste for the exotic and bizarre.

We caught the ten o'clock flight back to LA, and he drove me home, both of us talking nonstop about the great time we'd had. We hadn't been inside my apartment for five minutes before we fell into one another's arms and kissed long, hot, and deep. It was by far the most satisfying, wondrous, fulfilling kiss of my life! By this time I'd had a lot of sex with a lot of different guys, but none of them had rocked my soul like mild-mannered John Williamson! We began jerking off our clothes, trying to keep our lips connected as we tugged items of clothing over our heads and down our hips.

John's feet got tangled in his hastily shoved-down trousers, tripping him, and he pulled me closer, taking us both crashing down on the sofa. We were panting and gasping like horny teenagers, our hands moving hungrily over each other's naked flesh until at last he was inside me. We fell into perfect rhythm, thigh against thigh, belly against belly, my legs wrapped tightly around his waist, my breasts crushed beneath his chest. Our movements became faster, more frantic, and we rolled off the couch, crying out in simultaneous orgasm on the floor. We lay still for a moment, stunned, breathless, shaken, and then John ran a hand through his hair and said, "Wow! I haven't been this excited since the first time I got laid in backseat of Dad's old Ford!"

I collapsed against him in laughter, feeling an incredible sense of satisfaction. Not only was this the first time I'd experienced simultaneous orgasm, it was also the first time I felt so good and happy after having climaxed. Our joined laughter was as easy and natural as breathing.

We made love again, this time in my bed, and again it was mutually satisfying. It was hard to say good-bye when he left around dawn. He smiled down at me and said, almost casually, "If you're not busy tomorrow night, give me a call after work."

Of course I called and went directly to his place, a small, one-bedroom apartment he described as "just a place to sleep." The kitchen table and counter were littered with electronics parts for a new type of switch he was developing. And there were lots of books—stacks and stacks. Books on psychology, religion, sociology, science and science fiction, physics, psychedelic drugs, psychiatry—even a couple of current best-selling novels. I was impressed.

When we weren't talking, we were making love, and the evening flew by. Finally, as I was standing at the door reluctant to leave, John pulled me against his broad chest and murmured, "Why don't you bring some clothes over and stay here?" I was momentarily stunned. It took me a minute to respond. Then I sort of shook my head and mumbled, "No, I—I don't want to move in."

A couple of days later, however, I did just that. I had never felt happier in my entire life than I did living with John. I was no longer lonely, disconnected, and so hyperactive that I couldn't sit still. *So this is love,* I marveled. It really was rainbows and butterflies in the belly, a shortness of breath at just the touch of his hand on mine. We were so comfortable with each other, compatible both in bed and out, never running out of things to talk about. We worked hard and shared similar aspirations. The sex was great, but looking back, I think the easy companionship was what really rocked my world. I felt such a sweet surrender, a sense of belonging. It was like coming home but to a home I'd never experienced in real life. I felt safe and secure and confident with John. I'd always been very confident in myself, in my intellect, my business knowledge and strategy, my ability to set goals and reach them—but I had always been alone. I had never let anyone see behind the professional exterior and into the core of me. At that time of my life, I doubt I even knew who the real me was. My brain was always churning with questions—who, what, why, where, when? I never asked these questions out loud; people might think I was nuts, or just plain boring.

Not John. He listened and nodded and understood. He'd been asking himself the same questions. Why did we live in such an uptight world? Why was so much negative importance put on human sexuality? Gay, straight, bi—who cared? Married, single, divorced—why did it matter? Why did everything need a label? Why couldn't people just live together in peace and harmony in a world where jealousy and possessiveness did not exist?

In retrospect, I think the seed that would grow into Sandstone was planted in John's tiny apartment in 1966. For the very first time in life, I was happy—deeply, truly, completely happy—and it was a glorious feeling. Everything we did was spontaneous, and yet it all fell into place like the pieces of a puzzle. One night we were having dinner at the Hungry Tiger restaurant in the San Fernando Valley, talking animatedly, as usual, when John casually said, "You know, we should get married."

"Why not?" I shrugged. "I love a good challenge!" I know I sounded cool and hip, but inside my heart was pounding like a jackhammer against my rib cage. I had known this man less than a month, and here I was agreeing to spend the rest of my life with him.

For a man with a rather ponderous exterior, John moved very quickly in the next couple of days. He obtained a divorce through the American Consulate in Mexico City, cleared his calendar, and had his best friend George and his wife Joyce drive us to Las Vegas to tie the knot! We didn't care about a religious ceremony, and we didn't want a big fancy wedding when we had better things to spend our money on (like the new business we were starting), so we invited a small handful of close friends to be witnesses and to party with us after the deed was done. Quite frankly, we both agreed marriage was simply a means to satisfy the complex legalities of both our estates and any future business dealings we might have.

The ceremony was over so quickly, John didn't even get a ticket for double parking in front of the courthouse! Even though everyone was laughing and having a marvelous time, I realized I was shaking inside. We went to Caesar's Palace for a celebratory dinner and drinks, and when one of the girls mentioned the lack of a bridal bouquet, I stood, bowed from the waist, and ceremoniously presented her with my brand-new marriage certificate. "For luck," I told her. "You're next."

Everyone laughed and clapped and cheered as she accepted the certificate with the same enthusiasm as if it had been a dozen white roses. A sense of relief washed over me, and the shakes were suddenly gone. My silly little gesture had publicly reasserted my independence. John sat quietly, a benign smile of approval on his face.

When we returned home John moved his things into my apartment in North Hollywood. It was much larger and nicer than his place but still wasn't large enough for our combined belongings. I called a realtor, who found a perfect home for us on Mulholland Drive in Woodland Hills. It was almost completely furnished, which was great, as neither John nor I had very much furniture. It was beautifully decorated in delicious colors and cushy couches and chairs, everything tastefully and elegantly perfect. I was thrilled! The house was situated at the top of a small hill on a dead-end road and had a sweeping view of the San Fernando Valley. Looking over the valley at night could only be described as a spectacle—millions of flickering, blinking, multicolored lights far below like a handful of precious jewels tossed upon a backdrop of black velvet. Cathedral ceilings eighteen feet high surrounded a massive fireplace built of enormous native rocks, and in the kitchen was a built-in barbeque pit! The brick patio was built around a huge, towering oak tree so tall we couldn't see the top! It was like a gigantic umbrella and provided much- needed shade during the hot summer months. A master bedroom and two smaller ones completed the picture; we wasted no time moving in.

John and I sat and talked far into the night, planning the kind of life we wanted, the future that could be ours if we could only get our message out to others. But how would we do that? In order for someone to accept a new product or a new anything, there must first be a prototype to show them that it works. Our plan would involve changing the way the world looked at marriage and commitments and sexuality, at the ability to love openly and unselfishly. If a married couple could openly share their mates with others just for the sheer pleasure of it, if they could joyfully and freely have sex just because they wanted to and it felt good, then why not? It's kind of like you have this delicious, juicy, wonderful piece of cherry pie, and it's so good you want to share it with your best friends; and they have a scrumptious, creamy piece of chocolate cake—so you swap bites! Pretty simple, right? But how would we get that message out without jealousy rearing its ugly head, without that old killer possessiveness taking over? Pleasure makes our lives more exciting and fulfilling; however, there were pleasure police everywhere preaching that we shouldn't enjoy living so much. They wanted us to believe that hard work, the nose to the grindstone, the owning of possessions was the American Dream. Bullshit! Dreams are filled with pleasure. Who wants to dream about hard work and deprivation? So how would we get the word out?

"We'll teach by example," John said. "We have a lot of friends. Most of them are pretty open-minded, so let's just see how open-minded they are. What do you say, pumpkin? Are you on board?"

"All the way," I said. "Just blow in my ear, and I'll follow you anywhere!" He grabbed me and blew in my ear, and I snuggled against his broad chest, laughing and hugging him closer. That old reckless spark for adventure and danger flared up inside me. I was filled with a sudden thrill of excitement, a heart-pounding curiosity, and an eagerness to begin this unknown journey with the man I loved. Good, bad, or indifferent, I knew for a fact that this was the turning point in my life.

Our goal was to live an alternative lifestyle peopled with like-minded pleasure seekers. We knew that people fell into two categories: the inner directed or introspective, and the outer directed, who were all about pleasing others. It would be much easier to make personal changes and transformations for the inner-directed group, as they would want to please themselves rather than please others. But they would discover that in doing so, the pleasure would naturally encompass others.

Before we started bringing anyone else into our extended family, John assured me (many times!) that his life commitment was to me alone. We were soul mates with a strong primary bond, and above all we would continue to love and earn each other's trust. He assured me he would not allow anyone else to convince him that they could better serve his primary needs than me. "I solemnly promise you that I will never lose my head and allow anyone to lead me around by my cock!"

I didn't know it at the time, but John had already figured out exactly who I was and what I wanted. Hell, I didn't even know yet! "After our first weekend in San Francisco, I knew you were the one," he told me. "You were the perfect mate for Project Synergy. Professionally successful, independent, self-assured, sexually liberated—you remind me of Dagny Taggart, the heroine in *Atlas Shrugged*."

John saw me as the prototype of the new woman of the changing middle class and, in a synergistic sense, ideally suited for him. My assets complemented his deficiencies and vice versa. I was verbal and active, while he was theoretical and introspective, more direct and efficient if less calculating and visionary. I did not procrastinate.

We were both still toiling away in the highly stressful corporate world, so when John suggested a restful weekend in Lake Arrowhead, I was delighted. As we were packing for the trip, John casually mentioned that we would be stopping to pick up Carol, a young woman from his office. I knew who she was—a former airline stewardess, tall, curvy, and redheaded but certainly not an intellectual threat. Why the hell had he invited her? I didn't know the woman but had heard John speak of her several times. They had dated briefly and now worked together, but that was about all I knew. All of a sudden I felt my stomach churn with jealousy. Just the sound of this woman's name brought out the green-eyed cat in me. But I wasn't going to say anything. *I'll just sit quietly and see what develops,* I thought, but I already knew I would hate her on sight.

I'm not quite sure how it happened, but when we picked Carol up she slid into the front seat next to John, and I was relegated to the backseat! I was thoroughly and completely pissed and sat fuming in a slow-burning jealous rage for the two-hour drive to Lake Arrowhead. John and Carol seemed oblivious to my discomfort and chatted together like the old friends they were. Carol seemed to be genuinely happy to meet me and was friendly and warm, telling me how impressed she was by my success in a mostly male- dominated business. She turned in her seat often to try to include me in her conversation with John, but I stubbornly refused to be drawn in. I was mad and jealous, and I wanted her to know it, but secretly I kind of liked her.

When John had first told me we were taking her with us, I suspected that it was a test of sorts. I was being put in the position of either remaining on the sidelines with my insecurities and jealousy or joining my husband and Carol for a weekend of pleasure. This was John's way of showing me that open, wholesome sex with a friend need not disturb the deeper meaning of marriage.

When we arrived at the lake I was filled with relief when I saw that the cabin had two separate bedrooms. Some of the hostility left me as we went out to dinner and Carol continued to try to befriend me. But I was still a little sulky. I wasn't ready to give up my pout so easily. We went back to the cabin, and I almost fainted when John moved his and Carol's luggage into one of the bedrooms and left me sitting alone in the living room! John left the bedroom door open, and I soon heard the sounds of movement, laughter, and soft conversation and saw them casually begin to remove their clothes. I was stunned, shocked, and deeply hurt and just sat there, not knowing what to do. I tried to think clearly. The open bedroom door was obviously an invitation to join them, but I was paralyzed. When the sounds of their love-making drifted through the open door, I felt like an arrow had pierced my heart. I stood on shaky legs, dizzy and numb all over as I walked into the other bedroom and closed the door. I cried all night.

The next morning I was awakened by John's gentle kiss and saw Carol standing behind him holding a breakfast tray and smiling. Soon they were both in the bed with me, stroking, caressing, murmuring words of kindness, comforting me as if I was a small child. I was both grateful and embarrassed. I wasn't mad at them. John kept telling me how much he loved me and needed me, and I was filled with a strange contentment. I felt free—of what, I wasn't sure. I guess John had freed me of certain indefinable fears and romantic illusions about sex and body pleasure as distinguished from the meaning of marital love. The fact that my life partner had been engaged in sex all night with Carol didn't seem so shocking after all. He had expressed his love for me in front of her, and now there was no reason for lying. Just like that, our relationship became more honest and open and expanded for both of us. I realized I could do anything with whomever I pleased without risking his rancor. I was both stunned and stimulated by what had just happened. I was suddenly filled with a complete realization that I was married to a most uncommon man—mysterious, unpredictable, never boring, a quiet, thoughtful man who loved me dearly.

I needed to think. I didn't know if I wanted to forgive Carol (for what?) or befriend her. I took a long walk, and when I returned to the cabin, I showered, dressed, and went into the restaurant to look for them. They saw me and stood when I approached. Both of them hugged me, and Carol kissed my cheek and John kissed me long and deeply like the lover he was. There was a special warmth and a silent bonding between the three of us as we drank and laughed and enjoyed this time together. But John wasn't through with me yet.

"David, hello. Sit down," John said, and I turned to see a very handsome man standing next to our table. I recognized him as David Schwind, an engineer friend of John's. I'd seen him a few times before and had been attracted to his good looks and athletic body. He was part of a group of friends who'd gone water skiing together at Pine Flat Lake near Fresno a few months before. I remembered his strong but delicate features, his shy manner, and his terrific body—and I remembered how my girlfriends and I had whispered and giggled about how good-looking and sexy he was. He was thirty years old, never married, employed as an engineer at Douglas Aircraft, and just an all-around nice guy. But what the hell was he doing here? Then it hit me. *John, you sly old fox, you!*

David sat down, and we ordered another round of drinks, and, just as John had known it would be, my attention was tweaked by this handsome almost- stranger. I knew what John expected of me, and I was a more-than-willing participant. It was almost midnight when we returned to our cabin. David and I were so engrossed in conversation that neither of us noticed that John and Carol had slipped away. Then David suddenly said, "Hey, where's John?"

"Oh, he's with Carol," I said. "Don't worry about it." I was a little surprised by my newfound nonchalance as I placed my hand on his leg and gave it a little squeeze. "It's all right, David. We both want you to stay."

There was just a moment of hesitation; then I wrapped my arms around him and kissed him. His response was immediate and passionate.

Making love to David that night and again at dawn was a source of great release and unabashed pleasure. Far from having any misgivings about it or feeling romantically detached from John, I felt quite the opposite. I felt I had now achieved a new level of emotional intimacy with John. We had both shared during the night, in different rooms with different people, a gift of loving trust. Instead of loving him less after sleeping with another man, I loved him even more. The next morning when I walked into the small kitchen and saw John making coffee, I went into his arms, and he kissed me and held me close, giving me a soft smile of approval.

When we returned home, we did a lot of talking and soul searching. Even though we were blissfully happy together, we both realized we were very unhappy with our lifestyle. It seemed so shallow and meaningless. We were both making a lot of money, but it was sort of like being on a treadmill. We weren't going anyplace. We weren't growing as human beings. What we needed, we both agreed, was an alternate lifestyle, an existence that fed our souls rather than just our bank accounts. Instead of spending a fortune on designer clothes and shoes, wouldn't it be great to just go naked? If either of us became attracted to someone else, why push down the desire and hide it in shame? Why not go ahead and enjoy an occasional sexual encounter with someone else? That certainly wouldn't make us stop loving one another, especially when done with one another's full knowledge and approval. If you really deeply love someone, you want them to experience all the pleasures life has to offer.

The hippie movement had ushered in the idea of communal living—a group of like-minded people living together and sharing everything: money, food, chores, child rearing, philosophy, and so on. But those communes were usually quite humble, sort of living off the land. In most cases they managed without electricity or running water, eating only what they could grow in their gardens or panhandle from anyone willing to lend a hand or a few dollars, bedding down in sleeping bags, and wearing clothes they'd gotten from the local Goodwill or Salvation Army.

As John and I sat and talked, a vision was born. What if we started a commune, a grown-up one built with comfort and ease in mind where everything was beautiful and well kept, with a big, luxurious home that would comfortably hold as many guests as we wanted to join us. We envisioned lovely furniture, soft lighting, beautifully manicured lawns, well- tended grounds, and a clean, well-stocked kitchen with all the amenities of a perfect civilization. There would be no pettiness or jealousy, no possessiveness, just open and loving sexuality. High up in the Hollywood Hills as John and I sat and talked and planned, Sandstone was born in both our hearts. It was my destiny.

Chapter 4

DURING THE TWO YEARS WE lived on Mulholland Drive we fell into a sort of nightly therapeutic session with our core group of friends. We would sit outside naked in the warm California evenings having cocktails, passing a joint, and discussing the meaning of life and happiness. Bonding with the group was essential for all of us. John and I knew that to keep a heterosexual marriage or relationship together we must create a bigger one. We felt it was impossible for one man and one woman to fulfill all of each other's needs. From the first day, John had always accepted me just as I was. No one had ever done that before. He was warm, caring, sexy, respectful, and filled with a rare human kindness I had never experienced before. His IQ measured in the genius range, and he had chosen me as his life partner. The old doubts haunted me. Was I worthy of him? Could I keep him? Would he tire of me? Was my love enough? We had so many deep and meaningful conversations, and the only thing John ever promised me was that I would have an interesting life with him. I would never be bored. Now, over four decades later, I can honestly say he was right!

However, it took a lot of work. I had to completely rethink everything I had learned and believed to be true before I met him. I needed to learn how to love myself. If I didn't love me, how could I expect anyone else to love me? My parents had done such a number on me with their cold, distant attitude that I had grown up feeling unworthy of love. If my own mother and father didn't love me, then I certainly must not be loveable. John taught me this was absolutely untrue. During my many years with him, I experienced the deepest, most soul-satisfying love any woman could ever experience. That search for love and acceptance took me to Sandstone—and it was one hell of a trip!

While living on Mulholland Drive, we dabbled in group sex. The sex was playful, fun, energizing, bonding, and slightly serious in nature. John was so refreshing with his soft, smooth manners. He clearly adored women and was a master at empowering them. He told me more than once that he felt women should run the world because men were just fucking it up!

So I asked him, "Is the American Dream enough for you? I mean, look at us. We pretty much have it all. We both make a great deal of money. We live on Mulholland Drive, rubbing elbows with movie-star neighbors, driving a brand-new Jaguar XKE convertible, our closets filled with designer clothes, and we can pretty much do whatever we want. That's the American Dream. Is that what you want? Is it enough for you?"

"Hell no!" he said emphatically. "Our culture has such a narrow focus on making and hoarding as much money as we can that we've lost sight of inner happiness. What about spiritual enlightenment? What about fun and feeling good inside? We can make a lot more money, you and I, because we're smart and we know how to make money, but after a while it's just a big bore, because we are not doing anything different. We're in a rut. Like a rat on a treadmill, running faster and faster, making more and more money but with no time left over to enjoy life. We need newness in our lives. Difference is what keeps our creative juices flowing. It keeps us interested in the many joys of life. As for the American Dream, it's bullshit! I want a hell of a lot more."

My heart filled to overflowing. I had lassoed the moon and stars, and they were right there in my arms. "Let's do it," I said. "Let's shake things up!"

David was the first one to join us. He moved into the Mulholland Drive house and was completely onboard with an alternative lifestyle. The three of us discussed what kind of people we would all be comfortable sharing our lives with. Oralia, a rare natural beauty from Mexico, was a perfect choice. She and John had been friends for a long time, and she clearly adored him. When she met me, she extended that friendship and admiration, and we became great pals. She moved in next, and it just seemed natural that she and David would hit it off and pair up. For the first time in their lives they were seeing a possible opportunity to develop their primary relationship with one another in a supporting environment. Our family was beginning to grow.

We chose only upscale family members that were achievers and firmly entrenched in America's traditional values. Our family members were people that Middle Americans could identify with and relate to. It was about this time that I revived my sexual relationship with John Bullaro. He worked for the same insurance company, and we had kept our dates secret because we both had pretty high profiles and it would have been a huge scandal. He was married, but I was not; I hadn't met John yet when I first dated John Bullaro, and when I did and we married so quickly, I gave up my afternoon trysts with Bullaro. However, when John and I started gathering members for our extended family, he thought the Bullaros would be an interesting addition. He invited John to lunch and explained what we were doing and asked him if he and his wife, Judy, might be interested in checking it out. After that first evening, Judy was more than willing to become a part of our family—John, not so much. It took some convincing, but he finally did come around.

Next Arlene Gough joined us. She had been a friend of John's before I met him. She was pretty and very sexy and claimed to be clairvoyant, bragging that she could get anything she wanted. Except me! I was kind of leery of her from the start, but she wormed her way into the group and was there nightly. She claimed to make her car run on the freeway without gas. I really wondered how she did that.

I invited Gayle Williamson (no relation), an administrator of a hospital and a client of mine as well as a good friend. She was warm and friendly with a very kind soul and a good heart. In her early thirties, she'd never been married and hadn't had that much sex in her life thus far—not that she didn't want it, but in those days it was still frowned upon for a woman to be the aggressor. That was about to change, and Gayle loved it! She fit perfectly into our group. We now had eight people we could count on to be with us nightly, and we continued to interview others who came up regularly, but they couldn't really commit.

In the late sixties, swingers and wife swapping were all the rage, and we had a lot of parties but John and I were looking for a family to live and love together. Most of the party-goers were not interested in our goals and commitments—they were just there for the sex and then went back to their lifestyles, jobs, families, and so on.

During 1967, John and I decided this was it. It was now or never. We had a small group of friends who believed as we did and wanted to make changes in their lives. We had to find the perfect piece of property, and after we settled in, we could continue our search for more members.

John cashed out of his corporation in early 1968 with enough money to start us down a path of self- discovery, an exciting new social experiment. We began looking for property around the canyons in Los Angeles. We wanted space and privacy, peace and quiet. Finally, a realtor from Malibu showed us a fifteen-acre estate in Topanga Canyon. It was very secluded, quiet, and peaceful. Towering eucalyptus trees lined the long, curved driveway leading to a sprawling ranch-style mansion atop a gentle slope of tangled wildwood, bushes, and brambles. It was wild and unkempt but breathtakingly beautiful. The realtor told us it had been built in 1935 by one of the original land developers in Malibu to be used as a sort of playground for the movie stars of that era. In the thirties and forties, it was de rigueur for the rich and famous to have a special place they could go where the press couldn't follow. Many of the hunkiest leading men were in fact homosexual, and that knowledge, if it got out to the public, was a sure career killer. The same was true for the actresses, the ingénues who so perfectly portrayed the girl next door or America's sweetheart but were in fact wild party girls who drank and frolicked and loved sex. Sandstone had been built with privacy in mind. The long, winding, treacherous, narrow road leading up to the mansion was almost death-defying—especially after heavy rains had washed out the road and left deep ruts and potholes that jarred your teeth!

So in February of 1968, with cash in hand, we made an offer on the property. There was already an offer in place from the rock group the Monkeys, but before it could close, their manager skipped out with their money. Another rock band made an offer, but it fell through when the lead singer died of a drug overdose. That left us. Sandstone now belonged to the Williamsons. As we walked around the property taking notes on what needed to be done and what supplies we would need, the task seemed almost impossible. The large, terraced front yard was overgrown with bushes and weeds that all but obscured the beauty of the stone walls, and the roads and foot paths had been washed away by heavy rains. The house itself was neglected and dirty, with faded, old-fashioned wallpaper, spiderwebs, and cold hardwood floors. But John and I were visionaries. We saw it as it could be—and would be. John was from a hardscrabble farm in the South, and I was from a farm in Missouri, so we hitched up our pants, dug in our heels, and went to work.

Five of our best friends shared the same vision: Dave, Oralia, Judy, John, and Gayle. Their work ethic was as strong as ours, so they rolled up their sleeves and grabbed shovels and wash pails. The seven of us brought with us a shared communication theory, Ruth Benedict's synergy, the theories of Maslow, Chardin, and many others. We saw Sandstone as a perfect setting where those theories, as well as John's own, could be tested.

First, we had to make the place habitable. This required a complete renovation. We sandblasted the walls, bringing back the natural beauty of the wood; scrubbed windows until they sparkled; painted; and added crystal chandeliers, thick plush carpets, and all the amenities of a million-dollar retreat. John bought two bulldozers, and he and Dave cleared all the mud and debris off the road and driveway. It was backbreaking work. The hot California sun beat down, and we all sweated and sweltered in the unforgiving heat. Our only saving grace was the huge swimming pool that was sheltered inside an adjoining building. Ceiling-to-floor windows banked one entire wall, which overlooked the terraced yard and surrounding vegetation. At the end of a long, hard day, we stripped off our sweaty clothes and plunged into the cool water. It was heaven! (Later on, we would keep the pool heated to 93 degrees, near body temperature.)

Slowly, the transformation took place. The rough, shaggy, untrimmed bushes and trees took shape. The neglected house became one of elegance and grace with soft lighting and plush furnishings. I decorated with one thought in mind: Would the furniture feel good to naked skin? Would the deep pile of the carpet caress bare feet? Would the lighting flatter one's features? There was a huge room downstairs with a mammoth fireplace at one end, and we immediately dubbed it the ballroom and furnished it with several mattresses and water beds from wall to wall. Here, members and guests could engage in sexual play to their hearts' content. A nearby bathroom featured a double shower (for group showering, of course), and we decorated it with X-rated wallpaper. The wallpaper was really quite beautiful, a gold and white tangle of foliage and Art Nouveau curlicues that, when closely inspected, revealed happily fornicating Lilliputians. Every position of sexual intercourse was exquisitely depicted. None of us had ever seen anything like it, but we knew we had to have it at Sandstone.

John and Barbara

With each passing day as we all toiled and sweated, I began to be filled with excited anticipation. What would it feel like to actually live in such a place? I had only lived in modest dwellings before—a rather barren farm house, a small apartment in North Hollywood, a nice house on Mulholland Drive, but nothing fancy. Sandstone gave off an aura of richness, one of class and distinction, a warm, all-encompassing ambiance. We had worked like dogs to rebuild, add totally new extensions, tear down old and useless outbuildings, tame the wild tangle of chaparral, and coax blossoms out of the surrounding bushes and wildflowers that dotted the terrain.

The summer of 1968, we moved into our shiny new creation, just the five of us—Dave, Oralia, Gayle, John, and me. All of us agreed on the importance of environment. Everything, people and property alike, must be compatible and benevolent. However, Mother Nature didn't always play nice. The first year we lived there just happened to be the year of the heaviest rainfall that area had experienced in several decades. For a couple of heart-pounding days we feared the whole place was going to slide right off the edge of the plateau and into the deep Topanga Canyon. Luckily, the only casualty was our jeep. The five of us stood helplessly by and watched it slowly sink into a mud hole during one of the heavier downpours. But we were undaunted. When the rains ceased, John jumped into the bulldozer and cleaned up the phenomenal mess, and we forged ahead.

Next came the part of our endeavor that wasn't much fun but had to be done. It was mandatory that the property pay for itself. I had moved from sales into social engineering at my insurance company, but it was not going to be possible for me to straddle two worlds. I would have to quit my job and give up my incredible income—as would John. We had to figure out a way to make enough money for the upkeep of Sandstone. It required an enormous amount of work and cash to keep it as beautiful as we had made it. A few ideas were kicked around. We could sell shares or rent it out to movie studios, but none of us wanted a bunch of strangers tramping through our serene paradise.

"How about a membership org?" I suggested. "We can select enough people who feel the same way we do about life, people who are striving to accept and understand their own sexuality and to live a life of freedom from sexual restraints. We charge them a membership fee, which will cover the cost of food, utilities, and upkeep on the property. I think it would give them a sense of belonging, a sense of pride in Sandstone, and they will devote themselves to keeping it up and running. It will behoove them to keep their home away from home a place of peace and beauty. Sandstone will be their haven and sanctuary, where they can experience an alternative lifestyle free from bullshit."

THE JOURNEY OF THE MOST LIBERATED WOMAN IN AMERICA

Barbara, Dave, Oralia and John

John and I had often talked about a retreat from the harassment of daily routine, a place where we could embrace a nonconfining relationship. Wouldn't it be great, we said, to live in a spirit of family with several members who shared everything, who had divorced themselves from the inane, shallow cocktail banter with all its games and dodges and hiding behind the trendy trappings of the day. Once you remove your designer duds and stand naked in a group of other naked people, everyone is equal. "Give yourself permission" was our motto—permission to be yourself. Sandstone was a community, an environment that offered each member the chance to maximize their potential to unite mind, body, and being.

During this time, we had a rather unique encounter. A princess (who shall remain nameless) contacted us and inquired about Sandstone. Was it for sale? She was representing a group of Buddhists who were looking for property to turn into their own retreat. Intrigued, John agreed to meet with her and drove down to Studio City. He didn't come home that night, and I was frantic. For the first time in my life, I was filled with the most intense, green-eyed jealousy. I was convinced that he had fallen in love with the princess and I would never see him again. I paced the night away, and when he walked in the next morning I was torn between relief and fury. As I ranted and raved, he sat calmly, smiling that quiet, sweet smile of his and admitted that yes, he had gone to bed with her. Sputtering with frustration, I informed him that if there was another visit, I was going with him!

"Fine," he said, smiling. "That should be a lot of fun!"

There was another visit, and I did go with him, and it was fun! In fact, it was the most spiritual and exciting sex I'd ever had! It was my first sexual encounter with a woman, and I had finally discovered who I truly was: a bisexual woman happily fulfilled!

Those long, lazy, sun-kissed days of our first summer at Sandstone were magical. As we meandered through the winding trails naked, the sun warmed our bodies, turning them brown with health and vigor. We were recruiting possible members, and a virtual parade passed through our lovely mansion that summer. This was also the era of Timothy Leary, who encouraged his followers to "turn on, tune in, and drop out!" At Sandstone we did just that. The first thing to go, of course, was our clothes. Next were our inhibitions. We were all very curious about the psychedelic experimentation that seemed to be sweeping the younger generation. LSD, magic mushrooms, and mescaline were all readily available, and we embraced the chance to expand our minds and enter a new consciousness. Sandstone was a perfect environment to give ourselves permission to cross new psychological boundaries safely with a warm, trusting, intimate group of friends.

We had to be very careful in our selection of members. Anyone showing violence or aggressive tendencies was removed from the property immediately! That was exactly the thing we were removing ourselves from. Violence is the one emotion that kills any living environment, and it would not be tolerated. At Sandstone, a therapeutic environment was abundant, with everyone helping each other through moments of personal transformation. We often laughed about how much money we were saving on therapists' bills!

I wrote out a schedule that seemed workable. Sandstone would be open six days a week for relaxing, sunbathing, swimming, walks on the many wooded trails to enjoy the abundance of nature, chatting with other members, socializing, and taking advantage of the ballroom, which would always be open. Wednesday was potluck dinner night, and we also had party nights Friday through Sunday. Live-in staff members as well as John and I preferred to be nude at all times, and this helped new members to get more comfortable with their own nudity. It's funny how some women approached nudity. They would readily strip off blouses, bras, and shoes but keep on their jeans or a bikini bottom. Men would just drop their trousers and go commando as soon as they entered! Saturday was our big party day and night, and soon we were hosting as many as eighty attendees. As everyone became more comfortable with the environment, clothes dropped off more readily, and complete nudity was embraced by all. No one compared anyone to anyone else. ("Is his penis bigger than mine?" "Does she have a better figure than me?" "Are her breasts larger and firmer?") Watching others having sex minimized jealousy. Partners needed to be able to approach one another with honesty and in a mature fashion. There were heterosexual partners, bisexual partners, multiples, groups, and threesomes and primary and secondary relationships. I can't tell you how many times couples came to me and thanked me for saving their marriage, saying that their time at Sandstone had been better than a dozen years spent in therapy! On weekends, many guests and members slept over. There were a handful of small cottages just for this purpose as well as the wall-to-wall mattresses in the ballroom, so everyone had a soft place to slumber. Every night as darkness fell and the flames in the fireplace flickered lower, I would gaze about at the utopia John and I had created and be filled with indescribable joy. Everyone sat or lay in contented comfort, satiated with good food and drink, glowing in the aftermath of sexual contentment, happy and joyful. The camaraderie that filled the room was like nothing I had ever experienced before. The lonely little girl who was only seeking to love and be loved had found it in abundance. At those moments, I would glance over at John and find him gazing at me with that soft, gentle smile tugging at his lips, and I knew I had found my place in the world.

I'll never forget the day Marty and Meg Zitter showed up at Sandstone. They were from Haight-Ashbury, where they had experienced the whole hippie psychedelic movement. But what had started out as a peace and love association with young barefoot girls wearing flowers in their hair and young men strumming on guitars had turned dark and ugly. Innocent pot smoking and curious acid trips had turned many of the rudderless teenagers into desperate addicts who committed crimes to feed their habit. That one small stretch of Haight-Ashbury was filled to overflowing with kids who had left their loveless homes seeking a better life. With so many people filling such a small place, tempers flared and violence erupted as they all searched for their piece of space.

"It was time to hit the road," Marty told us. "We're looking for meaning and organization in our lives, a place where we can just be ourselves."

A look passed between John and me—Marty and Meg were a perfect fit for Sandstone. He came from a marketing and sales background, and she was working on her anthropology degree. It wasn't long before I began passing part of my workload to Marty. He was perfect for working the door and handling members. Open-faced, gregarious, witty, and friendly, he was a true people person and a real asset for Sandstone. Suddenly, we were being deluged with requests to go on television talk shows to discuss our way of life, and UCLA asked us to speak at group psych classes. Everyone, it seemed, was curious about communal living, especially at Sandstone, where we embraced open sexuality and nudity. To the outside world we were a "naked cult" or "just a fuck club," and that's where Marty's people skills came into play. He was a genius at fielding questions and handling the publicity that came our way. Our membership was quickly filling up with people from every walk of life:

entrepreneurs, religious leaders, academics, social leaders, film-makers, movie stars, attorneys, doctors, rock stars—anyone and everyone who was looking for an alternative lifestyle. It wasn't long before John began dealing with the press on a full-time basis. Word of Sandstone was spreading around the world. We received letters from many places in Europe lamenting the fact that they would never be able to visit in person, but they congratulated us on our new, bold approach. We ran ads in *The Free Press* and opened an office in Westwood to take calls and interview prospective members. This allowed us a chance to cull out the sex perverts (and a lot of those types showed up on our doorstep!) and to avoid the wierdos. We laid out our philosophy and were soon able to tell immediately if it was a good fit or not. We didn't create Sandstone to make money, but we needed enough to support it in the style we'd chosen. We needed eight to ten year-round, live-in members to meet the monthly overhead (food, utilities, paper products and cleaning supplies, drinks, etc.).

Our attorney drew up nonprofit papers even though we were pretty sure the IRS would not give us tax-exempt status and make it possible for us to raise tax-deductible donations. No others, including human growth centers, had ever done what we knew was imperative—unleash sexuality. And that meant stopping in at the Malibu Sheriff's Office and letting them know our plans and asking if they could patrol and protect Sandstone. They rather reluctantly agreed to patrol the grounds when convenient, and as time went on we actually formed a friendship with most of the officers. On Sunday mornings different officers would stop by and come inside for a cup of coffee and conversation. It was always a giggle to see these uniformed cops sitting with a group of naked people, catching up on their paperwork and simply enjoying the special ambiance that was Sandstone.

I had become so used to being nude that when I had to put on clothes to go into town for shopping or when the weather turned cold, it felt strange and unfamiliar.

Now that we were up and running, it became imperative that we find a live-in cook and housekeeper. I had absolutely no kitchen skills—nor did I want them! Oralia handled many of the indoor chores while Dave helped John maintain the grounds. It was a huge place both inside and out, so it took a great amount of work to keep everything bright and beautiful.

Once these mundane but necessary steps were taken care of, we were free to turn our full attention to enjoying the life we had created. After my romp with the exotic princess, my first female-on-female sex, I was a little surprised to discover that it wasn't that easy to find another sexual partner.

The women who came to Sandstone were sexually liberated, but they just had sex with men—several different men, but still just men. I couldn't find anyone who was open enough to have sex with me! However, that was before Raye drifted into Sandstone. Tall and slender, her skin toasted a golden brown by the sun, her hair a wild, sun-bleached blond, she was the definitive free spirit. From the first moment we met, I felt my heart lurch in my chest, and when she pulled me against her naked body and kissed me, all my senses soared. She flat out seduced me, and I was a more than willing participant.

No one else in the room (or the world) existed—only Raye and her lips, hands, and tongue, the sleek softness of her body, her total freedom, and her willingness to give as much pleasure as she was receiving. I was in love. For the next six months I floated in a daze and counted the hours until I could be in Raye's arms again. I didn't really know it then, but an exciting new process was in play within. Another whole world was opening up to me. I was no longer confined to relating only to males for sexual satisfaction. I was free! The orgasms I experienced with Raye and her magic tongue were the most amazing I'd ever enjoyed. We had sex many times, but she also had sex with several men. Her only goal was feeling good with whom she was involved. I knew she was irresponsible and a bit of a flake, but she gave me the confidence I needed to pursue women on my own. And then she was gone. Like a light, airy breeze, she just wasn't there anymore. Empowered, I was now able to search out women, and I was a little surprised to find them much more willing to explore same-sex encounters. At long last I was on the road to developing my own true sexuality.

Everything was going very smoothly in those early days. We had our staff in place, and most of our live-in members had been comfortably settled into their own cottages. John and I thought it was important for our family to be involved in a primary relationship. We didn't want a lot of single guys living there like kids in a candy store, waiting for the women to show up so they could have sex with them.

I think it was in the fall of 1969 that we first met Tom Hatfield. He had already been interviewed in our office on Westwood Boulevard, but he still wasn't sure what Sandstone stood for. I remember him saying he thought it was a nudist club, and he wanted to write an article about us. John hastened to inform him we were much more than just a nudist club; in fact, clothing was optional.

"We call it the Sandstone Foundation for Community Systems Research," John told him. "Our long-range goal is to form a large-scale community, a retreat from artificiality. The environment here has been very carefully and deliberately designed to promote human relations at all levels. Our members are free to just relax and do whatever they wish in a spirit of natural community and mutuality. Their unity lies in a deep-seated need for honesty, sharing, and freedom from bullshit. Yes, we do promote open sexuality but in a very relaxed, low-key sort of way. There's absolutely no pressure. No one is judging you. No one is keeping score. For the first time in your life, you are given permission to just *be*."

"I think I get it," Tom said. "You guys are trying to facilitate human relations and intimacies of all types and intensities within an atmosphere of dignity and love."

"We're not just trying, Tom," I said. "We're succeeding. Look around. Feel the peace. Our main goal is to form a bond with our fellow man. The Sandstone experience is a kind of search, if you will, for the possibilities of what communities might be—and should be." I noticed that while we were speaking, his eyes were darting around, trying to take it all in. We were in the living room, which, as I mentioned before, was very large and beautifully decorated. A huge stone fireplace dominated one end of the room, and there was a four-foot-high wooden planter filled with lush greenery that separated it from the dining room.

"Would you like a tour?" John asked. "Come on—let me show you around."

I saw Tom's eyes widen as he took in the eight-foot, glass-topped dining table surrounded by eight high-backed, beautifully upholstered chairs. A huge breakfront stood against one wall, its dark wood varnished to a high sheen. Everything from the expensive, tasteful furniture to the paintings on the wall and the plush carpeting spoke quietly of grace and elegance. Sandstone could easily have passed for a Beverly Hills mansion and just as easily could have graced the pages of *Better Homes and Gardens*. (I remember when we showed him the grounds he gave a long whistle of appreciation and said, "My God, I've never seen anything so perfect! There's not even a dead leaf on the driveway!") I found myself thoroughly enjoying seeing my lovely home through the eyes of a stranger. It gave me a new sense of appreciation, and I felt pride in my decorating skills.

We passed through the well-appointed kitchen with its dark wood cabinets and top-of-the-line appliances, and John opened the door to a set of rather steep stairs leading to the basement. The stairs were carpeted in deep, rich red and led us into the ballroom. "I guess you could call this our party room," John said. "It's where most of the activity takes place." Not only was the carpet red but so was the lighting. We had installed red lightbulbs in all the outlets, which gave everyone's complexion a soft, almost mystical glow. Very flattering! Wall-to-wall mattresses covered the floor, and there were a few small tables scattered about large enough to hold drinks and ashtrays. A bar stood against one wall and was backed by a large mirror, and there were several three-dimensional paintings that Tom stopped to peer at with a quizzical expression.

John laughed and said, "They make more sense when you're stoned!" Next was the beautiful gold and white bathroom with the fornicating figures in the wallpaper. Tom studied them for several minutes. "Very interesting." He grinned, and I saw a slight blush redden his cheeks.

"Let's go out this way," John said, opening the large sliding-glass door that led out to the driveway. The view was breathtaking. No matter how many times I saw it, I was always moved by its beauty. The canyon dropped off abruptly into a deep gorge that ran all the way to the ocean. It was early spring, and the hillsides were very green, dotted with hundreds of fresh new wildflowers that grew in abundance. We all just stood in silence for a moment, drinking in the peace and beauty. Tom was clearly dazed by it all, and John touched his arm to get his attention. "Come on, Tom," he said softly. "I'll show you the swimming pool."

"Huh? Yeah, okay," he responded. "Wow—this is too much. Far out, man."

"You ain't seen nothing yet," John chuckled, and we exchanged a private look, both of us thinking, *Wait until he sees the pool.* Double sliding-glass doors led us inside, and I heard Tom's sudden intake of breath. Cedar beams ran the width of the room, holding up the ceiling of fiberglass panels that allowed the sun to filter through. Large wooden planters held an array of lush greenery and banked the walls and windows, bringing the outside inside the spacious eighty-by-fifty-foot room, turning it into an intimate grotto. "We keep the temperature at about 92, 93 degrees," John told him. "It's very relaxing."

"I'll bet it is," Tom agreed. "Man, this is overwhelming—all of it. Everything." I noticed that his eyes slid over my bare breasts and down my body. John placed his arm lightly around Tom's shoulders as we all returned to the living room.

Oralia, our exquisite, dark-skinned, beautiful, and naked housemate, got drinks for everyone, and Tom couldn't take his eyes off her. Again, a private glance passed between John and me, and he grinned and said to Tom, "So, Tom, what do you think of Sandstone?"

"Where do I sign, and how soon can I move in?" he said, and we all laughed.

And that was how Tom Hatfield became resident manager and the first member of the permanent inner family to write a book about the Sandstone experience.

Chapter 5

UNLIKE THE REST OF US at Sandstone, Tom was always eager to make contact with the public. "Every new venture needs publicity," he explained. "I'd like to kick around the nonprofit angle, see if we can get donations from the members—I mean, above the yearly membership dues. If they love Sandstone as much as they seem to and want to keep the doors open, they should be able to come up with a few extra bucks. And the nonmembers, the people who just come up a few times for parties and such—they should be willing to contribute."

That was one of the things I admired about Tom. He was always thinking of ways to benefit Sandstone. In fact, he was the one who brought Gay Talese to our attention. It was one of those quiet, peaceful Saturday mornings when most members and guests were either still sleeping or gathered in conversation on the sun-drenched patio, sipping their morning coffee. The air was soft and still, a typical summer day in Southern California. John and I were sitting on the couch with our own morning coffee, talking about the party that had taken place the night before. We usually had lovely dinner parties on Saturday night and often ended up feeding a good sized crowd. When the phone suddenly rang, it sort of startled us, and John put his hand on my arm and said, "Relax, pumpkin—Tom will get it."

I watched as Tom spoke on the phone and saw an excited animation wash over his face. He was nodding and grinning, and I heard him giving directions to Sandstone. "Wow! You'll never guess who that was!" He plopped down in a chair opposite John and me. "Have you guys ever heard of Gay Talese? He's this big-shot very prominent journalist author, and he wants to meet you guys. He said he's in the process of writing a book about sex and just about everyone he interviews tells him he has to talk to John and Barbara Williamson at the Sandstone Ranch. He wants to see for himself what we're doing up here." His grin broadened, and he clapped his hands together with delight. "This could put us on the map, kids. I told him to come on up."

A couple of hours later I was shaking hands with Gay Talese. He was a tall, slender man dressed in brown tweed, an odd choice for such a warm day. I noticed that his shoes were by Gucci and his gold watch looked very expensive. His female companion was rather attractive but in a nondescript sort of way. She was wearing embroidered jeans and rather timidly stood just a little behind Gay as if using him for a shield. I invited them in and introducing them to John and Tom. As John engaged them in conversation, I gave Gay a close look: Olive complexion; dark eyes and brows; a rather sharp, hawklike nose; thin lips; tousled salt-and-pepper gray hair; a sort of wiry energy. He seemed to be the definitive fast-paced New Yorker, intent on business. However, when I made full eye contact with him, I saw a lively spark of mischievous warmth, and I liked him at once.

His date was obviously wealthy, dressed in Gloria Vanderbilt jeans, a silk shirt, and bejeweled sandals. She sort of murmured that she lived in Beverly Hills, and that's pretty much all the contribution she made to the conversation. Gay told us he'd heard about us from several people and that a good friend of his, Pat McGrady, said that if Gay was writing a book about sex, it was imperative that he visit Sandstone and talk with the Williamsons. We had once done an interview with Pat.

"We'd love to have you stay," John said. "Look around the place, meet some members and guests, and stay for dinner. Saturday is our big party night, so you can join in the activities or not. Whatever turns you on."

Of course, John, Tom, and I were nude, and as the members began to move about the grounds and inside the house, pausing to say hello to Gay, they too were nude. I noticed that Gay was making a valiant attempt to keep his gaze focused on each person's face rather than look directly at their genitals. It was kind of cute, and I gave him a conspiratorial wink.

Jo hn gave Gay and his date (I don't remember her name and never saw her again) a tour of the house and grounds, and I noticed that as the day wore on, Gay became visually more relaxed. Some of his big-city edginess and the tense lines between his eyebrows relaxed, and he was friendly and much more animated. During dinner he was outgoing, witty, sensitive, and very charming. He personally engaged each person at the table with sincere interest, and before the end of meal everyone was eating out of his hand. His charm and likeability seemed genuine, but I still wanted to wait a bit and see what he was like in the long run. I was only mildly surprised when his afternoon visit turned into a ten-day stay! I think the lady from Beverly Hills caught a ride down the mountain with one of the guests; I don't really remember.

During his stay, Gay made an appearance on *The Tonight Show* and told Johnny Carson all about his adventures at Sandstone. His most recent book, *Honor Thy Father,* was still on the New York Times bestseller list and he told Carson he was working on a new book to be called *Sex in America.* (It was published with the new title *Thy Neighbor's Wife* and became an instant best seller. Sandstone was mentioned prominently throughout.) During his interview with Johnny Carson, Gay raved about us and our lifestyle at Sandstone. "It's fantastic," he gushed. "Everybody walks around nude. There's a lot of touching and hugging and friendly kissing and the greatest feeling of camaraderie I've ever experienced! The lighthearted rapport between the members and guests is unbelievable. If you want to have sex, you simply take your chosen partner by the hand and lead them into the ballroom and have sex! It's that simple."

Johnny picked up his pencil, leaned in close, and pretending to write, asked Gay, "What was that number?" The audience roared with laughter.

Gay finally left, returning to New York City with a clear understanding of what Sandstone was all about and realizing the uniqueness of the people who lived and played there. I don't think he'd ever seen anything like it. He had taken copious notes and interviewed everyone he met, charming them with his intelligence and wit, but he still hadn't convinced John that he truly understood our mind-set. Some of the residents at Sandstone admitted to feeling a little uneasy around Gay, and some objected to his questions. I think I was still giving Gay the benefit of the doubt; I believed that he did indeed grasp the true meaning and the essence of the Sandstone experience. John didn't think so and continued to keep him at a distance. At first, John tried to communicate with Gay, but his style of straight talking seemed to threaten Gay, and Gay would often fly into a rage and stalk away. John's soft-spoken self-confidence, his unerring belief in himself, his refusal to allow Gay to ruffle his feathers, drove Gay crazy. He had a massive ego. He was used to getting his way. He had flattered, cajoled, and courted himself into the Beverly Hills and Hollywood crowds and enjoyed his celebrity as a best - selling author. He used his intellect as a weapon against those he considered unarmed. Looking back on Gay's first few days at Sandstone, I can understand how he must have felt. He was used to traveling in the rarified circles of the rich and famous, and they had all kissed his ass. But at Sandstone, he was treated just like everyone else. That small group of just plain folks showed only a rather detached interest in him, completely ignoring his professional status. Bottom line: no one was impressed by his celebrity, and it drove him crazy. Although I shared John's concern over Gay's perceptual abilities, I still instinctively trusted his drive and perseverance. I told John I thought he would treat us fairly, so we agreed to let Gay return and stay at Sandstone while he worked on his book.

Gay came back that fall with his belongings and a portable typewriter, and we set him up in a bedroom in one of the cottages.

We were crowded for space at the time, but the bedroom did give Gay the privacy he demanded. It didn't go well from the start. John's benign dismissal of Gay's celebrity and Tom's outright hostility over the communication problem, as well as the casual interest of the residents at Sandstone, crushed Gay's ego, often leaving him fuming and sulking. This was an experience he'd never encountered before. He was an outsider to this lighthearted group of insiders, and he knew he'd never be truly accepted.

One day, I suddenly decided I would attempt to personally bridge the widening gap between Gay and the others. I walked briskly up to the cottage door, rapped once, and walked inside. He was sitting on the sofa, his elbows resting on the coffee table, his chin cupped despondently in hands, staring out the window. Without a word, I went to him and enfolded him in my arms. With him in a sitting position and me standing, his face was buried in my breasts, and he let out a shuddering sigh. I could feel his pain and frustration as I pulled him to his feet and led him into the bedroom.

"Come on," I whispered. "Let's get you better."

I saw that his penis was flaccid, sort of dejected looking, and I slid down his body and took him into my mouth. I cupped his testicles in my hands, gently massaging them as my mouth worked its magic on his now fully erect penis. He was moaning with pleasure when I moved up and straddled him, taking him deep inside. "Oh my God," he gasped. "That's incredible! You love to fuck, don't you? So do I—it's my favorite sport."

Sport? I thought. *So that's where he's coming from. All right—I can relate and dig that ...*

For the next hour or so, we played and laughed and had sex in several different positions and talked, and for the first time I saw Gay without his public mask. I liked what I saw. Things changed after that afternoon. He faced Sandstone with renewed energy and a greater willingness to listen to its residents. His relationship with John and Tom improved almost at once, and they and the Sandstone family decided to give him another chance. Everyone agreed to be interviewed at Gay's request and to be honest and open. Although some people were still not convinced that he fully understood our viewpoints, they did believe he would treat us fairly and honestly.

The competitive undercurrent in Gay's relationship with John continued, however. I could see that Gay was jealous of John's ability to just be himself. With John, what you saw was what you got. No frills, no smoke and mirrors, just a happily secure man. We had a longstanding relationship with a delightful couple, Joan and Bud, and Gay picked up on that closeness and moved in on Joan. It was obvious that he was trying to take Joan away from John, thereby gaining control. It was childish and ridiculous, and of course it didn't work.

Gay also had a tendency to treat women as objects, denying them their full expression as individuals, and this didn't fly with Sandstone residents. He got together with several women at the ranch, but when the relationship started to turn more intimate than just a casual fuck, Gay immediately withdrew.

In spite of all the undercurrents, I became deeply committed to Gay's cause and introduced him to people outside of Sandstone who could provide him a better insight into the voluminous material he was collecting. We spent a lot of time together over many lunches going over his notes, comparing, discussing, and so on. I think I was also trying to compensate for John's casual dismissal of Gay's self-important celebrity. In that area, I was not successful. John was John. End of discussion.

My own conflict with Gay also revolved around a lack of communication. We never had a deep, meaningful conversation. Our relationship was strictly social—we enjoyed sharing meals together, exchanging our views and opinions, and discussing religion and politics, but I could never break through the mental barrier that said quite bluntly, "Gay is man. Barbara is woman." Constrained as he was by the deep patterns of our culture, he could never understand the concept that if he went into a restroom marked "Women" he would achieve the same result as he would have in the one marked "Men." He would still urinate.

It was another bright and sunny California morning when I met up with Gay having coffee in the main house. He asked me if I would like to come along and meet his friend, Bill Bonanno, the mafia son who was spending time in the Terminal Island Prison in Long Beach for some petty crime. I was thrilled to accept the invitation to actually meet Bill. It was a longtime interest of mine to meet someone in the mafia and unravel some of the mysteries about them. There was a mystique surrounding the mafia that perhaps prompted Gay to write a book titled *Honor Thy Father* about the top mafia family. I had to salute Gay for always putting his life in jeopardy to get a worthwhile story.

"We'll go to Long Beach for lunch." As much as I hated to put on clothes, especially on such a warm day, I slipped into a dress and sandals, and off we went. We took the back driveway that led to Tuna Canyon Road, a narrow stretch that snaked through deep canyons just west of the town of Topanga. Old water oaks and sycamores grew from the canyon's steep sides, and thick underbrush grew in the numerous small ravines dotted with wildflowers. Some of the larger trees leaned horizontally over the road, shading it from the furnace-like summer sun. Moss, ferns, chaparral, and a profusion of brightly colored wildflowers thrived among the huge, craggy boulders that had been left there centuries ago by the receding sea. No matter how many times I saw it, I was always struck by the sheer, raw beauty of those canyons. The wildflowers were awesome, a riot of vivid color and size, each one perfect and unique. Tuna Canyon Road had been laboriously dug foot by foot with pickaxes and steam shovels some forty to fifty years before, beginning at the coast of the Pacific Ocean and moving upward along the path of least resistance. It rose and fell, turning back on itself at times, more under the control of nature than its builders. At the worst blind spots, the road was barely fifteen feet wide. But it didn't seem to faze Gay. He expertly guided his rented LTD down this seldom-used road, chatting and gesturing, marveling at the panoramic beauty. Huge, vertical cliffs dropped straight down to the stream bed far below, and we could see the dazzling jewel blue of the ocean and just a glimpse of

Catalina Island off in the distance. This incredible portrait was framed by a tangle of gnarled oaks and scrub pines twisted by harsh wind and heavy rain over the years.

As soon as we turned onto the Coast Highway, we were engulfed by the heavy traffic and choking automobile exhaust fumes. This was one of the things I disliked most about leaving my mountain paradise. Our conversation died down as Gay navigated through the busy streets and into the Long Beach area. We had decided to have lunch at the HMS *Queen Mary*, an elegant ship that had been retired from the sea and turned into a lovely little restaurant. We were seated at a table with a porthole, giving us a nice view of sea and sky. Over cocktails our conversation resumed, and once again I was amused by Gay's smooth, glib way with words. By the time our lobster bisque arrived, I sensed that Gay was subtly turning our pleasant lunch into another interview. This time he seemed intent on questioning me about my childhood, wanting to know everything about my life growing up on an isolated, boring farm in Missouri. He was interested in how I had made the almost quantum leap from barefoot farm girl into high-ranking success in a man's world of insurance. I couldn't understand why he wanted to dwell on the past. Why didn't he want to know how I felt about my life today? What was it like being a free woman with free choice in a sexual wonderland?

I guess he sensed my withdrawal, because he suddenly changed the subject and turned on the Talese charm, telling me how wonderfully personable I was. "You are truly inspirational," he said. "When you speak, people listen. I watch you with the people at Sandstone. They all go to you with their problems, and you solve them simply and wisely. You know, you'd make a hell of good talk show hostess. You're like a female Johnny Carson. You're smart as hell, but you're also funny and easygoing."

I felt a puff of smoke being blown up my skirt! If I was as smart as he said I was, then why did he think I'd fall for his glib compliments? But I went along with it, pretending that his question was serious, and gave him a serious answer. "No way would I ever choose that lifestyle over the one I have now," I said. "The intense inner changes I've gone through, my complete dedication to the goals John and I have for Sandstone, and the peace and love in my everyday life far outweigh the glory of being a television celebrity."

"There's a lot to be said for celebrity." Gay grinned. "Lots of perks, lots of money, rubbing elbows with movie stars, riding in limousines …"

"True," I said, "but then I'd have to put on clothes." He threw back his head and laughed. "Touché!"

I was starting to get a little impatient. Knowing he would turn our lunch into an interview, I had carefully prepared answers to questions about sensuality, my new arrival at sexual independence, the impact male aggression had had on me, but I wasn't given an opportunity to express them. Gay's questions came right out of left field. He suddenly asked, "What did you do when that cop overturned his patrol car in your driveway?"

"What?" I vaguely remembered telling him about the time a police officer patrolling the area, had overturned his car in our driveway and had come knocking on the door for assistance. I had simply invited him inside for a cup of coffee while John and Dave fired up the bulldozer and righted his patrol car. I guess the visual was too much for poor ole Gay—a uniformed police officer, fully armed and helmeted, casually sitting on the sofa surrounded by a roomful of nude people, some of whom were having sex, was just too scandalous for Gay. "You know, Gay, that's just silly stuff. We should be talking about a need to abolish the twisted double standard that women have had to deal with most of their lives." That got us back on track, and we spent a pleasant afternoon discussing philosophy and other topics of interest.

When we got back to Sandstone, Gay went directly to his room without so much as a good-bye, but by this time I realized that he was often curt and rude, so I merely shrugged and went inside. I couldn't wait to get out of my clothes and into a nice, hot bath. I felt sticky with city grime.

Toward the end of his lengthy stay, Gay could no longer postpone the onerous task of interviewing John.

He had to, of course, because John was Sandstone. I could sense Gay's uneasiness around John, because John wasn't the least bit impressed by Gay. He had always treated Gay with the same open friendliness as he treated everyone, but he held himself just a little aloof—which Gay took as an insult to his intelligence. During his many interviews with members of Sandstone, Gay had always preferred a one-on-one conversation, but he wanted me present when he met with John. For moral support, I suspect. Gay also insisted that these interviews take place in various Malibu Beach restaurants rather than on the grounds of Sandstone. John much preferred to sit out in the sun and listen to a breeze ruffling the leaves or the sound of a bird singing while he talked and exchanged ideas. I think it was a power play with Gay; he wanted to get John out of his comfort zone and into his territory—populated, public restaurants. In any event, the locations for the interviews really made no difference at all. John was taciturn and rather listless in response to Gay's questions, which drove Gay crazy. He had seen how John reacted to everyone who visited Sandstone—with warmth, charm and charisma—but with Gay, he remained coolly detached. Then it suddenly came to me. John was reacting like a woman would react to an overly aggressive, pushy bully. I took Gay aside and told him he was approaching John the wrong way because "John thinks like a woman."

Flabbergasted, he yelled, "What the hell does that mean?"

I explained how John felt about women, and Gay digested the information for several minutes. "Okay, we'll see about that. I have an idea." He made a telephone call and set up an interview between John and Cynthia Sears, a well-respected female writer. When she arrived, I smiled at her professional suit, trim shoes, and matching purse—very much the way I used to dress when I worked in the business world. Her manner was calm and cool as she set up her tape recorder, her smile warmly friendly as she accepted a cup of coffee and made herself comfortable in one of the outside lawn chairs. A light breeze ruffled her hair, and she sighed and raised her face to the sun for a moment. Her whole approach was such a radical departure from Gay's journalistic sense of propriety, his macho pushiness, and John's response was instantly positive. Within a few hours of taping, Ms. Sears had effortlessly extracted all the important material that Gay had been searching for during his long stay at Sandstone. Throughout the entire interview, Gay wore an expression of disbelief.

When he was finally gone back to the hustle and bustle of New York City, I sighed a deep, long sigh of relief. The whole experience had exhausted me. I wasn't seeking publicity or celebrity, but I recognized the importance of it, because it helped to contrast our alternate lifestyle. It was the invasion of privacy I objected to. It would have been so easy for Gay if he had simply let go of control and blended in with the family; then everyone would have trusted him. We cringed at all the money Gay had spent taking us out for expensive dinners when he could have been a hero to us by diverting that money toward some badly needed funds for Sandstone expenses. We had a great chef willing to prepare dinners for us all.

Chapter 6

THE LOS ANGELES AREA WAS often referred to as "Shake and Bake"—first earthquakes would shake it, and then raging fires, fueled by the hot Santa Ana winds, would bake it. These hot winds would cook the air, expanding it, spilling it over the mountain passes. When conditions were just right, this hot, dry air flowed under a blanket of cooler air moving eastward from the sea. It became compressed and gained velocity as it is pushed downhill toward the coast, reaching gale force. The Santa Ana winds became as hot as a furnace, and all it took was one tiny spark of sun against a dry leaf to set off an out-of-control forest fire. Because it was a densely populated area, the fire quickly spread into residential neighborhoods. Everyone dreaded the end of summer and the threat of those hellish Santa Ana winds. As the lazy days of August slipped away, I noticed that the air had become heavier, the heat oppressive. Nothing moved. When I gazed across the terraced lawn, not a leaf or twig fluttered. Everything was as still as a painting. The last of the midweek guests had left for their homes in the city, and only the Sandstone family remained.

It was about four in the morning, and I tossed and turned, trying to sleep in spite of the heat. Splashing sounds from the pool and the last sighing orgasm had ceased a couple of hours before, and everyone had retired to their own sleeping quarters. Windows were flung wide open in hopes of catching even the slightest breeze from outside. Earlier that evening we had watched the news on TV and had learned that one of the largest brush fires in the canyon's history was moving slowly toward us from the east, burning its way through age-old trees and underbrush. The smell of smoke drifted through my open window, and I felt my heart thud with fear. I jumped out of bed and rushed outside. Several family members were already there, standing together on the lawn and watching the roiling black smoke float up from the canyon floor. The sharp, acrid odor of burning greasewood assaulted our nostrils. Perspiration broke out on our naked bodies. The heat from the Santa Ana winds swirled around us like a gust from a devil's fan. I don't remember what was said or if we even spoke at all. We just piled into the jeep with Michael behind the wheel and drove up the steep, narrow dirt trail that John and Dave had roughed out with their bulldozers. We stopped at the top and looked down into the pit of hell. Red and yellow flames danced in the darkness, sending long flaming fingers clawing at the stars. The fire appeared to be larger and closer than it really was, dwarfing the landscape.

We huddled together there in the dark, arms around each other's waists, hands gripping hands, and no one said a word. Then, almost as one, we turned and looked down at Sandstone. Its softly illuminated lawns and terraces and the silvery eucalyptus and ghostly jacaranda trees shimmered in the smoky blackness, giving it the look of a magic kingdom in a Disney movie. Wisps of smoke and the surreal colors of the wildfire softened its contours, and it seemed to float and waver like a mirage. All of a sudden, Michael leaped up on a boulder and faced the fire, the lean lines of his body and his long, shaggy hair silhouetted by the flames. He let out a rebel yell, shaking one fist at the sky. His other fist held his penis, and he defiantly pissed in the direction of the fire!

We all just stared for a moment and then broke into laughter and applause. That singular, primitive act released us from our shock and fear, and still laughing and high-fiving each other, we returned to

Sandstone to await the dawn. A couple of the women cooked breakfast, and every coffee pot we owned stood perking on the countertop. Every news channel on TV was broadcasting the advance of the fire, and a general order was issued for everyone in our area to evacuate immediately. A look of solidarity passed between us: we would not leave Sandstone.

Fueled by caffeine and adrenalin, we got busy packing boxes with personal papers, deeds, tax records, photographs, special souvenirs, and so on. We uncoiled every hose we had and placed them at the ready on the lawn, checking the water level in our huge storage tanks. They were all full, thank God! John turned on all the sprinklers and began saturating the lawn and terraced front yard. We parked all our cars, trucks, and jeeps facing the exit driveways for a quick retreat if it was necessary. Throwing on a pair of shorts and a blouse, I rushed down the mountain to our neighborhood grocery store and bought enough food to last a week: canned goods, crackers, cheese, energy bars, cereal, milk, soft drinks, anything that could be eaten without cooking, as we anticipated a lengthy power outage. The telephone was ringing off the hook as members and friends called to offer help or just to check on us to see if we were all right.

John and Dave took the bulldozers high up above our property and began cutting firebreaks all around, scraping away dry growth and pushing dirt down the steeper slopes. The temperature had soared to over 110 degrees and the work was gritty and backbreaking, but they didn't stop until we had a dirt trench surrounding all the buildings. Smoke swirled and enveloped John as he rumbled back into our driveway, and then it separated enough for us to see a patrol car screeching to a stop. The smoke was so thick we hadn't seen its approach. An officer flung open the car door, raised a bullhorn to his mouth, and ordered, "You have to get out of here! Evacuate this property immediately! Now! Move it!"

"No fucking way!" John yelled back.

"Yes you will, goddammit! That's an order!"

"We don't take orders at Sandstone." John leaped down from the bulldozer and walked toward the officer. He was naked and covered in dirt and soot.

The cop's mouth dropped open as he stared at John and then raised his eyes to the rest of us standing in the driveway. We were equally nude and covered in dirt and soot. He saw the determination on our faces and in a weary, resigned voice said, "Okay—I can't force you. Just be damn careful, you hear? If the fire gets too much closer, you have to get out. Your property isn't worth your life. Got it?"

"We're taking all precautions, officer," John said and stuck out his hand. The officer shook it, and I saw his eyes sweep the naked breasts and bodies of the women. I caught his eye for just a brief second and gave him a saucy grin.

By early afternoon, most of us had cooled off in the pool and were sort of milling about, keeping an eye on the TV. Since the power was still on, we cooked dinner that evening, and by nightfall we were all feeling much better. Exhausted and still a little frightened, we hung out together in the main living room, enjoying cold cocktails and conversation. Not knowing what tomorrow might bring, I don't think any of us slept that well.

John and I were the first ones to step outside and survey the damage. The sky was black with smoke, and there was a thick layer of ash covering the ground. Flames were visible to the north, near the tennis court, and the tut-tut-tut of helicopters could be heard overhead. Canadian fire-fighting planes had been recruited for the emergency, and they roared overhead, dumping tons of sea water along the fire line. Helicopters just barely skimmed across the peaks of the mountains, releasing retardant chemicals from their bellies. Road blocks now completely isolated Sandstone. It was us against the demon flames. We stood on the balcony and watched police and fire-department vehicles wending their way slowly up the narrow roads. Bulldozers were clearing firebreaks on some of the other hilltops. Suddenly, from out of the thick smoke, several fire-department pumpers climbed ponderously up our narrow driveway and into the courtyard. A fire captain, his face and blue uniform streaked with soot, jumped down from the cab and called a greeting. We were all gathered together in the driveway, and we enthusiastically returned his greeting.

"Glad to see you folks are all right," he said. "Would you mind if we set up a base camp here?"

"My God, yes—please do!" John exclaimed. "Just tell us what you need.

We have more water here than the county, if that helps."

"It sure as hell does!" the fire captain replied. "There's no more water in these mountains. All the lines are dry."

I reached out to shake his hand. "Just make yourself at home," I said. "Let us know if we can do anything to help."

As all the firemen piled out of their trucks, I had to smile at their astonished expressions when they realized that we were all nude. "What is this? Some kind of nudist camp?" one of them asked, and I grinned. "Something like that ..."

In just a few minutes, they had their pumpers connected to our water system and had spread heavy canvas hoses all over the grounds. Standby crews were summoned, bringing the total number of firemen to around fifty. We gave them complete access to the main house, and by mid-afternoon they had turned it into a barracks with sleeping bags covering the floor. Fire-fighting equipment was stacked by the front door, ready to be snatched up at a moment's notice. The fire line nearest us smoldered within its boundaries until a long flame suddenly shot out and spread to the terrain separating us from the ocean. We were now surrounded on three sides by the blazing inferno. Moving silently and grimly, a group of firemen held it at bay, turning the flames away from Sandstone.

There was a group sigh of relief, and one of the firemen said, "Man, that pool sure looks good. Mind if we take a dip?"

"That's what it's for," I said. "Have at it." A whoop of joy filled the air, and a dozen or more firemen began shucking off their heavy, bulky uniforms, kicking off their boots, peeling off their gloves, and heading for the pool.

Laughing and slapping one another on backs and buttocks, they flung themselves into the water like a bunch of carefree boys. They had been playing in the water for several minutes when their captain showed up. He stood in the doorway to the pool building for a few minutes watching his men relax and revive themselves in the healing water. I was watching him, wondering if he was going to order them out of the pool and back into their uniforms, when he sort of shrugged and dropped his own grimy, soot-covered clothes on the floor and dove naked into the pool. A roar of approval greeted him as he bobbed to the surface.

"Excuse me, ma'am—Ms. Williamson." A young police officer approached me and said there were several people at the road block claiming to be members of Sandstone and asking to be let through the blockade.

"If it's all right with your department," I answered, "I see no reason why they shouldn't be here with us." Within a few minutes about a dozen or more of our members showed up, and as was the norm upon entering Sandstone, they removed their clothes and began mingling with the firemen and police officers. One by one, they plunged into the pool, and a few of the couples started having sex together at the pool's edge. I noticed that several of the female members were eyeing the hunky firemen, so I wasn't surprised when they were soon engaging them in sex. I'm pretty sure that every fireman was well and happily serviced that afternoon; the members of Sandstone showed them the real meaning of hospitality.

It was late in the evening. Everyone had enjoyed a wonderful dinner. Wine and cocktails were available for those who wished to partake. I caught a whiff of marijuana smoke and saw that a joint was being surreptitiously passed around. Exhausted, I leaned against John, and we were both quiet as we listened to the animated conversation that swirled around us. The oddly mixed group of people had come together intimately and comfortably, and a bond had formed between us all on that one fateful afternoon. It could just as easily have gone the other way, I thought. Everyone could have panicked and turned on each other, but instead they had all pulled together and stood together as a family. I was filled with peaceful tranquility. This is what the world should be like. This is the kind of community we should be living in.

Around midnight, one of the policemen—I think he was a captain or someone in authority—spoke to some of his men, and it was time for them to leave. Some of the family members chose to go with them, and I admit I was sorry to see them go. What well could have been a disaster (and still could turn out to be, I supposed) had been a wonderful meeting of new friends. Everyone had a good night's sleep, not knowing what tomorrow would bring. As soon as I stepped outside the next morning, I saw the fire chief peering over the edge of the front lawn down a sheer, four-hundred-foot drop to the bottom of a heavily wooded ravine. Thick black smoke still darkened the skies in the distance, but now wisps of white smoke rose up from the ravines. Apparently this white smoke was more ominous, and the chief was clearly worried. He was holding a cup of coffee, and he walked up to me and said,

"I'm going to have to move everyone out. The whole damn canyon is going to blow. Until that ravine caught, the odds were with us, but now there's not a whole hell of lot we can do. All of you folks should leave as quickly as possible."

I heard movement behind me and turned to see the Sandstone family, those who lived there year round, crowded together. Each face held a look of determination. I laid my hand on the chief's arm and gently shook my head. "We appreciate all you've done for us. You and your men are the best. I doubt we could have made it without your help these last couple of days, but we're staying."

"No, Barbara. Don't." He covered my hand with his. "It's too dangerous." "Sandstone is our home," I said. "We—all of us—have poured blood, sweat, and tears and you wouldn't even believe how much money into this place. It's our life. We can't just walk away and let it go up in smoke."

He sighed and shook his head. "You know I can't force you, but for God's sake—"

Just then a small ravine near the main road exploded. Billowing smoke followed by a tremendous blast of roaring flames covered the hillside about a half-mile away. Telephone poles alongside the road ignited, flared up, and toppled over. The firemen sprang into action repositioning the heavy canvas hoses, pulling some of them to the edge of the cliff and spreading others across the lawn and terraced grounds. They told us to stay away from the house. At the first rush of smoke, we should jump into the pool and stay there. And then they were gone, disappearing into the heavy black unknown.

We all rushed into the pool building and stood on the steps trying to see through the smoke, but it was impossible. Then we heard it: a deep, bellowing rumble that belched smoke and debris, sending burning sparks in all directions. The tiny sparks flared into flames for a second and then went out due to the heavy saturation of the grounds. The constant soaking with the sprinklers had done its job; the grass and bushes were too wet to burn. The flames were arching over Sandstone and igniting the mountain behind us.

The threat was over. Not a single bush or tree was lost—not even those edging the mile-long driveway. Every flower, every shrub, every blade of grass remained intact. Aerial photographs taken after the fire showed the rectangle of Sandstone, green and lush, glistening in mile after mile of burnt, blackened destruction. The firemen had no explanation. I did. It was the magic of Sandstone.

For at least a full year after that devastating fire, visitors to Sandstone told of wending their way up the narrow canyon roads and seeing the black, charred remains of the once-lush vegetation that had spread as far as the eye could see. Where once there had been a sea of wildflowers, coarse grass, and alfalfa bushes, there was now a meadow of charcoal and ruin. Topping a small knoll that led to our driveway, the vista suddenly changed into one of color and beauty.

It's like *The Wizard of Oz,*" one visitor gushed, "when Dorothy sees the Emerald City for the first time! It's awesome, man!"

Things always slowed down a little during the winter months. It was too cold to stroll nude outside, and even indoors a lot of us wore clothes to ward off the chill. Both fireplaces burned day and night, fed by the cords of wood John and Dave had gathered in the fall. For me, it was a time of contemplation, of inner searching. I was still trying to form the real me, the whole package of Barbara Cramer Williamson. I had learned I was bisexual, that I could experience just as much joy and sexual satisfaction from a woman as I could from a man.

I remembered Gay Talese had called me "the most liberated woman in America" and had praised the work I was doing at Sandstone, but I still felt he had not captured the true spirit of what both John and I had really accomplished. He held a rather distorted notion about casual nudity and open sex. To him, and to almost all reporters who wrote about us, there was something naughty going on at Sandstone. They couldn't fully grasp the concept that sex is a socially integrating force of such scope and magnitude that it is often overlooked by our existing culture.

In spite of social evolution, sexual revolution, and liberation movements, the basic dilemma of men and women continues. Unable to reach an understanding, we resort to war tactics. We lay siege to those we love, attempting to conquer them and add them to our store of possessions. "My wife" and "my husband" are conceptualized the same way as "my car" and "my house." Wife, husband, car, house—all are mine, because I fought the battle and won them. No one likes to lose, so we all get caught up together in this struggle of conqueror and conquered. This same primitive conflict has been going on since the beginning of time. The boundaries of war and sex are the same. Whether religious, political, territorial, or whatever, the real conflict is buried in our primal consciousness—the fear and confusion about our sexuality. Males are viewed as aggressive, competitive warriors ("I came, I saw, I conquered"), and women have always stood by their men, supporting these beliefs.

I believe women are the most highly evolved creatures in nature, uniquely and naturally predisposed to establish the necessary balance in the crucial male-female relationship. By shirking the responsibility of their own sexuality, they have contributed to the chaos and pain that exists. I chose to cross that boundary, and I learned that the crossing itself was not chaos but what was on the other side. In some ways, my experience was like that of the racist policeman who suffered through such turmoil and rage while watching his wife have sex with a black man—and found peace and acceptance on the other side. That was always my goal: to find peace and joy and to leave behind all the turbulence and pain. Luckily and happily, I didn't have to make that journey alone. I was accompanied each step of the way by John, whose early research provided the theoretical foundation upon which Sandstone was built.

Throughout our many years together, we shared many wondrous adventures, solved many of life's problems, and carved a niche out just for us. Like a character in the old Tammy Wynette song "Stand by your Man," John always stood by his woman. His belief and pride in me gave me wings and allowed my ideas to soar. Together, we recognized the validity of our theories and worked to enlighten others. The implications of these findings ran in direct opposition to the old cherished myths about love, family, and religion, so we had our work cut out for us. Everyone who came to Sandstone was searching for their own personal fulfillment, because the rules and regulations in the rest of the world just were not working for them. They wanted the freedom just to be who they were—not labels like secretary, attorney, cop, CPA, doctor, housewife, barista, waitress, construction worker, etc. and so on. Those labels described their careers, not who they were as human beings.

My own experiences at Sandstone changed my life forever. It was there that I experienced the greatest sexual changes in myself. I discovered I was bisexual, and I embraced that knowledge, and it freed me and fulfilled me. Some people believe that if a person claims to be bisexual it's just a selfish cop-out, a license to have your cake and eat it too. If you're bisexual, you can have sex with both men and women guilt-free. Well, of course. That's what sexual freedom is all about. Whatever floats your boat! True liberation means freedom from guilt, loneliness, possessiveness, and fear. That path leads to becoming a whole human being, your own person. As Polonius says in Shakespeare's Hamlet: "To thine own self be true."

Chapter 7

THROUGHOUT MY TIME AT SANDSTONE, I dreamed of having a relationship consisting of John, me, and another woman. This combination can be the most stable, powerful, and synergistic of all relationships. Such a relationship also is one of the most difficult to maintain due to our current culture, which has proclaimed that the only normal sex is heterosexual sex—performed in the missionary position, of course! As recently as the 1960s, oral sex was against the law. Unbelievable!

But we didn't have any laws at Sandstone, so I continued to search for the perfect, permanent arrangement. Quite frankly, I was surprised at how difficult that was to find. It seemed that every woman wanted her own man. She might be open to having a three-way with another female, but when she closed her bedroom door at night, she wanted to be the only one cuddling with "her" man. Most men would jump at the chance to have two females in their lives and beds. It was the women who balked at the suggestion. This is not to say that I didn't experience many deep and meaningful sexually fulfilling encounters with women while at Sandstone, but I just never found the perfect partner for what I believed could be a perfect marriage.

From earliest childhood, there was always a sort of restless curiosity inside me. I was always searching for answers to the hundreds of questions that swirled around in my head. As soon as I discovered the answer to a particular question, I moved on to something else that intrigued me. Often my memories would go back to my lonely childhood, and I would be filled with sadness and loss. I would remember that the only happy times were those spent in the woods away from our house where I had befriended so many woodland creatures. Squirrels, birds, rabbits, raccoons, and even bobcats came to accept my presence and lose their fear of humans. I couldn't wait for spring, because that was when the mothers would bring their young out of dens and burrows and introduce them to the big, wide world. I saw the concern and care these wild mothers showed their offspring, always standing guard against any danger that might arise. The mother bobcats were the most ferocious of all. When I was lucky enough to catch a glimpse of a mama and her cubs, I sat as still as a statue so I wouldn't frighten them away or, worse, incur mama's wrath. That was really hard, because I yearned to scoop up the cubs and cuddle and kiss them.

So I had to content myself with my own domestic cat. When she had kittens, I watched in awe as she immediately began to lick and cuddle each kitten. Apparently not satisfied with where she had given birth, she found a different, more comfortable, and safer place for them in the corner of my bedroom closet. Grasping them by the scruff of their necks, holding the squirming bundles between her strong teeth, she moved each one to their new home. For the next several weeks, she licked, suckled, stroked, and drew them into the warmth of her body while they grew stronger. When she had to leave them to feed or relieve herself, she left them safely piled together, sleeping soundly.

From that moment on, I was fascinated with felines. I was especially drawn to big cats—tigers, cougars, lions, bobcats. I yearned to have one of my own, not just one I could look at from across a meadow or inside a cage at the zoo. I wanted to feel their fur, explore their bodies, check out those lethal -looking claws and fangs, put my arms around them, and feel the muscles hidden beneath their thick, glossy coats. That little rebellious, risk- taking spark inside me that responded to danger and excitement was still alive and well. I wanted to own a big cat—not as a possession but as a member of my family. I wanted to raise one, share my space and my love with something so beautifully wild, and what better place to do it than Sandstone? We had fifteen acres of wilderness, and I envisioned myself exploring them with my pal at my side.

I wanted to get a young feline and raise it like a child, a member of my family. I wanted to prove that bonding between species was possible. Maybe it was because I couldn't find the perfect woman to bring into my marriage with John that my thoughts suddenly turned to bringing a wild cat into the fold. Felines and women are more similar than one would think. Both are sensual, nurturing, protective, and dangerous when confronted but loving and gentle when treated with kindness.

Things were going so smoothly at Sandstone that I admit I was a little bored at times. I needed a new interest to fill me with excitement. I needed a bobcat! Topanga Canyon was a perfect place for a bobcat to live, as they were indigenous to the area. Obviously I couldn't go searching through the canyon, peering into dens, hoping to find a mama and her litter, so I approached it sensibly. John and I bought a new motor home and took to the open road in search of a bobcat. We left the care of Sandstone in the capable hands of Marty and Meg, Dave and Oralia, Frank and Terri, Albert, Michael, and a few other trusted family members, knowing they would protect it in our absence.

I had done a lot of research and decided North Dakota would be a good place to begin our search. Luckily, we had to go no farther than the Bismarck Zoo. We just boldly walked into the office and asked the man in charge if he knew where we might purchase a young bobcat. The guy was clearly surprised by the request, but he grinned and nodded. "Yes, as a matter of fact, I do—right here." He led us around back, explaining that their female had given birth to a male cub but hadn't been able to produce milk to feed it. "Some of the kids from 4-H have been taking turns feeding him by hand, and he's growing into a pretty feisty little guy! Cute as a button too!"

"How old is he?" I asked.

"Just turned three months," the guy said. "He's a friendly little fellow. One of the gals has been taking him home with her most nights, so he's used to being handled."

A young girl, about fifteen or sixteen years old, was holding this squirming bundle of fur when we entered the enclosure, and a few other teenagers stood or sat nearby. John and I approached, and all of a sudden, the young cat pulled away from the girl and leaped into John's arms! He wrapped his front legs around John's neck and straddled his waist with his long, gangly back legs. His paws were huge, and I reached out and touched one, stroking it gently for a moment. He turned his head and stared directly into my eyes, making instant contact. I was floored. I had read that big cats never made eye contact unless they were going to attack, but this little guy was looking at me with friendly curiosity. I moved my hand up to stroke and scratch his ears, and he butted his head against my hand, clearly wanting more. To this day I can't explain the emotions that swept through me. The closest I can come is probably what a mother feels when she sees her baby for the first time. My entire being was awash with love.

It didn't take long to take care of business. We paid the guy $250, loaded the bobcat into our motor home, and hit the road. He was perfectly comfortable and content riding in a vehicle, and once we were on the freeway, he sat up with those huge paws on the windowsill and watched the terrain fly by. I had begun to think of him as PC—Pussy Cat the bobcat—and the name stuck. At that time he weighed about fifteen pounds, and he would reach a solid thirty-five pounds as an adult. He was leash trained, so when we pulled into campgrounds for the night, I walked him as easily as one might walk a well-behaved dog. He was a perfect little gentleman, padding along at my side, never once pulling or tugging at his leash. Every so often, he would turn that magnificent head and look up into my eyes, and I swear to God he smiled at me!

I quickly learned that PC had a mischievous streak about a mile wide. One of his favorite tricks was to squat down behind the camper's curtains, and when he heard footsteps approaching (other campers walking by), he would leap at the window and scare the hell out of them. Apparently, this was good bobcat fun!

When we returned home, everyone made a big fuss over our new Sandstone member. The delighted exclamations, the reaching out of hands to touch and pet PC, the little squeals of fear from some of the women, upset him, and he pressed himself against my legs, looking anxiously up into my face. I scooped him up and carried him back to the motor home. Obviously, it wasn't going to work if we let him roam around free. There were just too many people coming and going at Sandstone. PC might get nervous and bite or scratch someone. There was also the danger of him straying too far away from home and encountering a coyote or rattlesnake. He'd been raised in captivity and was as gentle as a domestic cat.

There was a large slab of concrete just above the main house where an old dilapidated barn had once stood. John and Dave had torn it down months before with plans to build another cottage for our year-round members. "How about we park the motor home up there," John suggested. "Just until we decide what to do about PC's permanent living arrangement." The view was exquisite, overlooking Malibu beach and stretching all the way to Catalina Island. In the evenings, a string of sparkling lights flickered and shone along Santa Monica's coastline. It was quiet and peaceful.

I didn't want to just park the motor home on the hill, close the door, and leave PC all alone except at feeding time, so John and I moved in with him. We left our large, plush master bedroom in the main house and moved into the twenty-five-foot-long motor home to keep PC company. It was the most joyful, wonderful experience of my life. I was responsible for this young life. It was up to me to keep him safe, to teach him manners, to show him love, and to accept and respond to the love he showed me. Every morning the three of us would drive down the winding mountain road to the main house for breakfast. We had a little VW Beetle, and it was soon dubbed "PC's Bug," as that was usually his mode of transportation.

As mentioned before, our living room was sixty feet long, a great expanse where a young bobcat could race back and forth and stretch his growing body. There were usually a handful of people sitting around the living room and dining room drinking coffee, waiting for breakfast, catching up on gossip, and so on. PC would lie in wait until he saw someone holding a cup of coffee, and then he would pounce, swatting the cup out of their hands. Most nudists do not find it pleasant to have hot coffee splashed on them! But PC was just so damned cute and irresistibly funny that no one could stay angry with him. Just think of a domestic kitten—how playful and mischievous it can be—and then multiply it by one hundred, and you have PC!

He would leap from sofa to chair to sofa effortlessly, flying through the air with a look of pure glee on his little furry face. God, how I loved that cat! I enjoyed the pranks he pulled as much as he did. I remember when Gay Talese was staying at Sandstone and one morning he walked into the kitchen all decked out in a crisp new Beverly Hills white tennis outfit, looking like a rich playboy from an old Hollywood movie, and I saw PC behind a chair, eyeing him. He raised his nose, sniffing—picking up the scent of brand-new clothes, I suspected, which was a pretty alien scent at Sandstone. Then he made his move, leaping directly in front of Gay and swatting the cup out of hands, splashing the pristine white of his tennis duds.

It saddened me to see some people who were afraid to reach out to this playful little cub. I thought it spoke volumes about their character. He was just a baby, full of happy energy and curiosity, and I wanted him to grow up surrounded by love and acceptance. Keeping him separated in his own motor home and away from the less enthusiastic members was my way of making sure that when he was around people, they were only those who understood and appreciated him. He did spend a lot of time in the main house, and often others would join us on our walks, so he had his own circle of friends. He also had John and me sleeping with him every night, making the bond stronger.

Although I loved everything about him including his bobcat sense of humor, he had one habit that was totally exasperating—he woke up at 5:00 a.m. every morning, and when PC woke up, so did I! He made sure of this by running the full length up and down my body, standing on my chest, and peering into my face until I opened my eyes. So what if it wasn't even dawn? The boy was hungry and wanted his chicken. So I, grumbling and still half asleep, gave the boy his chicken! Later in the morning, he got a can of healthy, nutritious cat food and sometimes a raw egg to keep his coat shiny and give him some more protein. The boy may have been a little spoiled, but he was also very beautiful.

On Sandstone party nights, I loaded him into the VW, drove down the hill, and parked in the driveway of the main house where he could see the guests arriving. I left the window partially open, and when guests walked by, his paw would come shooting out to take a playful swat at them. He truly did enjoy being around people, especially women. He had a steady stream of adoring admirers, and he ate it up, but he also made it perfectly clear that I was his number-one girl. He did this by humping my leg every chance he got! And he loved to snuggle and cuddle. After the day's activities were over and John and I were in bed, PC would crawl up between us and settle in for the night. We would usually smoke a couple of joints and listen to music to help unwind, and PC would put his little wet nose right up against my lips, breathing in the marijuana smoke. He loved music, especially the theme from *The Godfather*. His tail would twitch and his big paws would sensually knead the blankets, thoroughly enjoying the powerful, haunting beat. I like to read at night, but when PC came into my life, books went out. He would position himself between me and my book, gazing up into my face as if to say, "Why do you need a book? You have me." Then he would purr that deep, rumbling, contented, self-satisfied purr that vibrated throughout his entire body. I was hooked, and he knew it. It was also evident that I would always need to have an exotic cat in my life. There was just something about them—their wildness, their uniqueness, their capacity for love—that could never be duplicated by any other species, including humans. I shared my life and love with PC for twenty long, glorious years, and when he passed away from a heart attack, he took the biggest part of my heart with him.

Chapter 8

WHEN I DECIDED TO WRITE this book, I wanted to give other family members a chance to tell their stories. All of the live-in members were profoundly changed by the Sandstone experience, and each of them wanted to tell about their own feelings in their own words. I wanted to start with Marty Zitter, since he was the closest we ever came to having a manager at Sandstone. I asked him to type up his memories and feelings and talk about how his life had changed; this is what he had to say:

In January, we (Meg and I) saw a small notice in the notorious *Los Angeles Free Press*, an underground alternative newspaper founded by our delightful friend-to-be, Art Kunkin. It listed a phone number of an office in Westwood, which I called. A man with a Bavarian accent named Albert invited us over to chat. Within minutes of our meeting, he gave us both a big hug, took a twenty-dollar guest fee from us, and provided a map to Sandstone along with an invitation to visit that Saturday evening.

The road to Sandstone is a two-lane, steeply rising, blindly curving piece of driver and vehicle torture. At night, as you pass over narrow ridges and around sheer outcroppings, you get brief glimpses of the sparkling city lights below. One last piece of tough road, and you enter the flagstone-lined courtyard of the remote mountainous estate carved in broad terraces from the native sandstone. In front of you is the expansive hacienda-style main lodge; to the right the redwood building enclosing an Olympic-sized swimming pool; and beyond acres of lawn, gardens, dozens of old eucalyptus trees, and several residential buildings.

We parked and entered the lodge and came face-to-face with a nude, voluptuous, gamine pixie of a woman who delivered a firm handshake and introduced herself as Barbara Williamson. There were perhaps twenty other nude people in the large, plush, beam-ceilinged salon as she brought us over to the great raging hearth to meet her striking blond, blue-eyed husband, John, and another handsome couple named Dave and Oralia.

Barbara took us on a tour of the place, where we witnessed for the first time in our lives copulating couples and coupling multiples virtually everywhere we looked: in comfy, dimly lit corners of the salon; dozens in the red-carpeted, mirror-lined ballroom on a lower floor; some in front of that room's fireplace; several on blankets on the front lawn under a full moon; and bunches in the dense fog of the heated indoor pool. Despite the forgoing, words cannot describe the sights and sounds including choice rock 'n' roll coming over the elaborate hi-fi, the moans and groans and shrieks of orgasms; and laughter at the clever commentary of a few pleasantly waggish participants.

The Journey of the Most Liberated Woman in America

Sandstone Ballroom

It appeared to be almost exclusively heterosexual among the men, with women acting as buffers between them or engaging in consensual lovemaking for their mutual enjoyment. Barbara steered us toward the unisex dressing room and told us to make ourselves at home; then she tactfully excused herself and left the room.

We stood there for a moment facing rows of neatly hung clothing with lines of shoes and duffel bags on the floor below. We peered back out of the room and saw adult humans ranging from eighteen to around fifty years old of varying sizes and colors, mostly quite fit and attractive, wandering in and out and greeting us and one another with smiles of joy. In moments, our clothing and shoes joined the inventory, and off we went, hand in hand, both with big smiles on our faces and I with an enormous, throbbing erection.

We stayed together that evening, savoring the spectacular Sandstone environment, and wound up on one of the gold velour couches in the spacious upstairs salon wrapped in plush towels and rapt in deep conversation with two other couples who had been members for several weeks. We talked with a couple married thirty-seven years and another on a blind date. Suddenly, we noticed it getting light outside. We had been up all night and had no idea of time or of fatigue.

At the far end of the room were a large dining area and a long formal table. We watched as several individuals carried pitchers of juice and milk; a coffee urn; plates and tableware; and trays of pastries, bagels, and eggs benedict to the flower-laden table. In a flash we realized that we were famished and leaped to our feet to join the already lengthening queue. Oh, the tastes and odors! Breakfast was never so good.

We walked outside onto the southern balcony of the lodge and first realized the remoteness of the place. There were just a couple of small houses below and well over a mile away, with the road beyond them. To the east the sun was rising over a rocky ridge; on the west was a steep, scrub-lined slope; on the north was the distant Sandstone Peak above; and to the south was a wild, 1,700-foot- deep canyon with the Malibu coast and the Pacific horizon beyond. Then it hit me. The totality of this intense night of open sexuality, at least in this first instance, felt to me just like a liberating peak experience during a well-guided, well-tolerated, consciousness-expanding psychedelic experience, of which we had had many. As Timothy Leary had taught us, one's emotional set and the protective physical setting of the trip had to be meticulously planned. Just then, Meg turned to me and said, "What a trip!"

The Sandstone brochure was startling and straightforward. In part, it read: "The strength and lasting significance of the Sandstone experience lies in human contact divorced from the cocktail party context, with all its games and dodges and places to hide. Contact at

Sandstone includes the basic level of literal, physical nakedness and open sexuality. In these terms, the experience goes far beyond any attempt to intellectualize it. The reality of action with its effect of accepting and being accepted is basic terms, without reservations, without cover, is the essence of the Sandstone experience."

What Meg and I found at Sandstone then was a residential intentional community of ten persons: five open couples, two of them married, living this philosophy but not without trial and difficulty. While the interpersonal problems between two persons are often daunting, the prospect of ten was staggering. We were soon to make it twelve.

The community's main source of support was the club and retreat programs through which everyone entered Sandstone. At first, we and two hundred other couples paid $240.00 per year and $10.00 per visit, $20.00 for sponsored guests, breakfast included. Later, special Saturday night dinners and week-long residencies were added as concessions. Beer and wine were permitted as BYOB, but drugs of any sort and insensitive, insistent, or intoxicated behavior were strictly and unequivocally prohibited. The members were also occupationally diverse. We met factory workers, clerks, nurses, scientists, teachers, business executives, actors, rock stars, a famous African explorer, a judge, and no end of writers and film makers.

The brochure went on to say, "The concepts underlying Sandstone include the idea that the human body is good, that open expressions of affection and sexuality are good. Members at Sandstone may do anything they like as long as they are not offensive or force their desires on others."

Unfortunately, it was not that simple.

Meg and I discovered that we were not immune to that emotion that we commonly refer to as jealousy. Our first involvement was with Barbara and John, the founders of Sandstone, who were six and nine years older than Meg and I. Barbara was bisexual and made demands on Meg, something Meg had not anticipated but came to embrace. I experienced anxiety for her welfare and for my own equanimity. She told me that she had had a feeling of frustrated possessiveness and a sense of separation or loss while seeing me make love with another woman. I felt the same way about seeing her come to orgasm with another man right beside me.

These feelings illustrated for us the knowledge that we could never really own or belong to one another. After a few weeks of membership, we backed off and went over what had happened to us. We were confused yet elated, more desirous of each other than we could imagine. Our ambivalence seemed not from the nature of the experience itself but from the heady newness of it. We decided that whatever happened, we were loving individuals in a special relationship that would always take primacy and remain inviolate.

We returned and talked at length with Barbara and John. We really liked them. Our conversations were warm and loving, and we were warned about head tripping or trying to rationalize too much. We were told to give ourselves permission to change and accept the realizations of our fantasies as ultimately our option. The real understanding of what happened would come with time and further exploration. Again, I could hear Timothy Leary and Aldous Huxley talking but also Abraham Maslow and Fritz Perls: "I do my thing, and you do yours. I am not in this world to live up to your expectations and you are not in this world to live up to mine. You are you and I am I, and if by chance we find each other, it's beautiful."

In the early 1960s, John Williamson, an inventor and self-made businessman, came to the conclusion that many of society's ills existed because people were alienated from themselves, from those they supposedly loved, and from their social environment. Wanting to do something to address this perception, he and Barbara sold their homes and invested their life savings in rebuilding the seriously distressed Sandstone Ranch property. The opening event, that blowout UCLA Halloween orgy in 1969, was described to us as a shock beyond even their wildest plans.

Meg and I visited often during the next few months and gradually became more involved with the people and organization. In May 1970,

Barbara walked us over to a small slightly flood- damaged cottage near an edge of the property and asked us if we'd like to do a little work to fix it up and move in permanently. Meg would help her with the day-to-day management and I, due to my gregarious personality, would take over membership development and be the official spokesperson. Meg finished up at UCLA, I quit NCR, and we packed up and were living there by the first of June.

We became fully involved in all the problems and joys of daily living in a large, loving family of intelligent, dynamic individuals. During long weekday evening conversations we learned the backstory of Sandstone—John's travels, former high-tech NASA career and prior marriage; Barbara's Midwest upbringing and success selling life insurance; their tempestuous meeting and affair with one another and with another founding couple, John and Judy Bullaro; and other formative events and characters.

We also personally shared all the chores of keeping the place up. I enjoyed watering and pruning the vegetation and raking up truckloads of the constantly falling eucalyptus debris. As I was very good with the french knife, I volunteered to slice, dice, and julienne all the fruits, salads, and veggies for the buffet. I may have invented the notion of cutting firewood with a chainsaw while in the nude, and John taught me how to run the Caterpillar tractor we used to keep the trails open after storms, and we all shared in the shopping.

My official job was interviewing and signing up prospective couples for membership and collecting the fees. Being something of an audiophile, I managed the all-important music system and subtle lighting for the parties. Members would bring new hit records during the day, and I would carefully program them to ninety-minute cassettes for our automatic changer, alternating ballads with upbeat dance numbers. Knowing this sequence and the mood I had designed frequently aided me in my own seduction plans.

Two of our frequent visitors were a lovely paralegal named Ellen and her attorney husband, Mark. One Saturday night while a slow song was playing and people were circulating, Ellen and I, both nude, crossed paths in the middle of the salon floor. Spontaneously, we began a slow dance and both quickly became aroused. As it happened, we were similarly proportioned, and our legs were precisely the right length to permit effortless intercourse as we kissed and gently swayed to and fro. Arthur Murray might have smiled.

Meg and I became involved with a delightful young couple that had recently moved to LA from Salt Lake City, Utah. They had been raised in polygamous Mormon families and had rebelled against the authoritarian structure and fled. The irony was that their upbringing had prepared them very well for the Sandstone experience. For several months we were inseparable as we frolicked and slept together in our king-sized bed.

There was also a serious side. Sometimes our Monday-night community meetings became heated, with jealousies and rivalries often erupting. For never having been trained as a therapist, John proved to be the consummate arbiter and peacemaker.

Sandstone started receiving good publicity from reporters coming to visit, and I began going to colleges and civic organizations to explain our work. Having been interviewed on TV by Tom Snyder and others, I achieved some notoriety, which helped in getting new members. The local sheriffs and especially the hunky, handsome LA County firefighters were now our best friends. We occasionally even invited the charming, well-behaved local Hell's Angels. Then came the celebrities, actors, entertainers, movie stars, superstar academics—too numerous and too many names to drop in such a short article.

It may have been too good to be true, because that's when the troubles began.

On August 2, 1970, the Los Angeles County Board of Supervisors adopted an ordinance aimed at Sandstone and Elysium requiring a ten-dollar license to operate a "growth center," defined as a place where "three or more persons, not of the same family, congregate for the purpose of exposing their bodies in the nude." On October 7, we went in front of the County Public Welfare Commission to request a license and were denied as a "detriment to the public welfare"—and they filed a criminal case against us. The crowd, resembling a lynch mob, chanted and carried picket signs out front, such as "No Nudes Is Good Nudes" and "Sandstone Must Atone," and overflowed the large hearing room. (I won't bore you with any more of the infuriating details. If you'd like to know more about the case and successful appeal, e-mail me and I'll send you the press coverage.)

Just a few days later the fires came. For two weeks we were closed down and beset with flames from all directions. The County Fire Department saved us, and we awarded each of them an honorary membership. Four of them later went on to make good use of it. But nobody was coming up anyway—many thought we were about to be raided and that they would all be carted to jail and booked as perverts. Our income seriously dropped off.

We never fully recovered. By the middle of 1971 we were hanging on and growing the membership, but John and Barbara's capital had all been spent on the case and keeping us afloat, and operating costs were going up dramatically. But the place looked good, the community was thriving, and the parties were rollicking. Filmmakers from San Francisco named Jon and Bunny Dana set about planning a documentary about us, and an author from New York named Gay Talese visited to interview us for his book about sex in America. Then we hosted Dr. Alex Comfort for several months as he researched his *Joy of Sex*.

In September, Meg told me she was leaving with one of the film crew and wanted to go back to school and pursue her career in teaching. I went to the closet and began packing to go with her, and she told me I couldn't; I had to stay and keep Sandstone going. I collapsed in tears, and she held me and then she left for San Francisco the next day. Meg became a heroic, award-winning paramedic and then went on to chair the science department at a gifted high school. She has since retired and heads a private science academy.

My next love, the girlish blonde Sue Bottfeld, was also a student (of philosophy), which eminently qualified her to help run Sandstone. Our situation was unique in that we had met there and had experienced the straightforward openness of the process from the beginning. We learned many things about our jealousy and possessiveness.

We never reached out to others during our periods of tension or adjustment. When the feelings were good, we were secure in our outside explorations. We insisted on getting to know our lovers together, generally not sexually but as friends and open confidants. It was important that others completely understood our relationship and would not be surprised or hurt by its primacy. There remained a gnawing feeling of distance and being left out that occasionally showed up. There was no way to alleviate that as far as we knew. We all feel it and wonder at it. Only a sense of personal worth and sure knowledge that we are indeed secure in our love helps to diminish this emotion.

In a pyrrhic victory, famed First Amendment attorney Stanley Fleishman prevailed for us, and on April 16, 1972, the Court of Appeals, Division 3, ruled two-to- one that the county regulation violated the First Amendment and that "operating a nudist camp [sic] is an exercise of the right of free speech." Ever the perfectionist, Fleishman was disappointed because he had rather wanted a ruling based on the right to assemble.

By the end of 1972, most of the original group had gone, and the writing was on the wall. Sandstone was sold to a dicey rehab operation, and Sue and I moved back to Santa Monica. John and Barbara bought a large motor home, refunded money to make the last members whole, gave us a generous portion, and headed to Montana, finished with Sandstone. I kept the books and records, hoping that one day they might prove useful.

In late summer 1973, Sue and I were walking around the Third Street Promenade when I heard my name called out from behind. I recognized the caller as Paul Paige, a psychologist and former Sandstone member. Paul came running up to us breathless and began saying that he had been looking for Sue and me for months. He went on to say that he and several partners had raised capital to buy Sandstone back, remodel it, and reopen it the next spring. He intended to raise the fees as well. Were we interested?

Yeah, we were! We got busy contacting several thousand former members and guests and visitors and putting together a mailing list. After a long and difficult escrow, which closed on Christmas Eve, Paul's lover Theresa Breedlove and I went up the next day in her pumpkin-colored Corvette to take possession. As we parked outside the lodge, we could hear the remaining rehab patients screaming and arguing. To our great relief, the last few of them emerged and drove away. We then began the massive cleanup effort.

June 1, 1974, was set as the official gala reopening date. It would be called "A Day with Gay (Talese) and an Evening of (Alex) Comfort," both being high-profile supporters of Sandstone. We would also have the charming and witty Theresa, the eminent Dr. Sally Binford (Meg's former UCLA anthropology professor), *Playboy*'s Nat Lehrman, and *Screw Magazine* publisher Al Goldstein on the dais to present to a crowd of some three hundred what turned out to be an outrageous and hilarious seminar in everything you ever wanted to know about group sex, comparative genitalia, and female sexual arousal.

We planned a music and art extravaganza by the brilliant comedian Orson Bean, who had given Sandstone the nickname "Cum -a-lot" and, in his best Richard Burton tenor, sang; "Cum-a-lot, we cum a lot, that's how conditions are ..."

The Los Angeles Times covered the event in a straightforward manner under the headline "Open Sexuality Reopens at Sandstone."

Sandstone began again, better than ever, but this time with a full menu of programs and workshops to bring in revenue beyond the membership. We were now attracting a large number of therapy professionals, including psychiatrists, who wanted to enjoy Sandstone for themselves and to refer client couples who they thought might benefit from the experience. We offered a full day-time residential program and courses with names like Gestalt Training, Bioenergetics, Rolfing, Pathways to Sensuality, Tai Chi Chuan, Sensual Massage, Touch for Health, and that perennial favorite, Naming Your Sexual Personalities.

Paul had promised us that Sandstone would be chartered as a nonprofit research institute so that we could seek grants and permit membership and referral fees to be tax deductible and that he would draft a long-term lease to the corporation that would give us an option to buy the property. That, I thought, would establish Sandstone in perpetuity.

But it was not to be. After much discussion, Paul tearfully informed us in spring 1976 that his two silent partners had run into financial problems and had already sold the property to a private- party developer and that we had to be out by year's end. Sue and I moved back to Santa Monica, and for us Sandstone had met its final end.

Sandstone closed just prior to the advent of the horrors of the HIV/AIDS era. Notably, during its entire time of operation, not a single case of sexually transmitted infection or disease was reported to us or even, by virtue of almost universal use of the pill, one case of unintended pregnancy. In recent years, the egalitarian term *polyamory*, which means "many loves," became more popular, and people continue living alternative lifestyles.

Until all those inconvenient, party-pooping aliments are finally vanquished, prospective polyamorists must bear in mind the essential precautions of understanding the known risk factors, using condoms and helpful STD testing services like SafeSexPassport.com, and the even more demanding interpersonal group dynamics of poly-fidelity.

I kept in touch (sporadically) with Marty throughout the years. He eventually went back into sales (he was very good at it!) and made quite a lot of money in stock brokerage sales and commercial property. He still cherishes his time spent at Sandstone. He and a new life partner settled down in Pasadena, California; bought a huge mansion; renovated it; and live very comfortably these days. When I spoke with him last year, he said he was working on a script for a movie about Sandstone.

As I mentioned earlier, there were literally dozens, perhaps hundreds, of reporters, journalists, writers, TV hosts, and movie and television producers scrambling to meet with John and me, asking for an interview and, of course, an invitation to Sandstone. Hundreds of articles were written about us, with and without our permission—so many that they soon became repetitious. I've always been a strong supporter of diversity, so when Marty told me about a lesbian couple, Margo St. James and her life partner, Pam, I was immediately interested in meeting them. Margo was a writer and wanted to do an article for the magazine *Sexual Freedom*. I gave Marty the green light, and he invited them up that weekend. I liked them both at once. They showed just a little uneasiness when confronted by forty or fifty nude people (as did everyone on their first meeting), but soon they were as relaxed as everyone else.

Margo's subsequent article was spot-on; she understood what Sandstone was all about. Here it is in its entirety:

Sandstone refers to itself as a retreat from artificiality—and indeed it is. Monastery-like in its setting high in the wooded hills of Topanga Canyon in the northernmost part of Los Angeles County, it offers a welcome retreat from smog and concrete to fresh, clean air and rolling hills with the ocean beyond, a retreat from city sounds to sylvan silence; a retreat from tension and bustle to lounging in the sunshine; a retreat from uptightness and compartmentalization to a new kind of community where a person's mind, body, and being are no longer strangers to each other.

My companion, Pam, and I arrived at Sandstone one Saturday evening as guests of a member, Marty Zitter, who met us at the door and informed us we were just in time for dinner. Since he and everyone else there was nude, Pam and I took off our clothes, too. It was a very natural thing to do.

Dinner was served buffet-style on an elegant period piece dining table at the far end of the spacious (60 foot long), plush-carpeted main living room. About twenty people sat around on the velvet couches and chairs or in front of the huge stone fireplace, partaking of a delicious, abundant, home-cooked meal of cheese fondue, artichokes with butter sauce, green salad, beef stroganoff, and pineapple chicken.

The conversation was light; people were friendly and outgoing. Pam and I began talking with a couple of interesting people—a TV director who was making a full-length pornographic movie for general distribution and a black dentist from Los Angeles who told us, "my wife and I come here every weekend. We like the peacefulness and relaxed freedom. There's no pretense or intellectualization of human emotions at Sandstone."

As the evening progressed, more people arrived. By eleven o'clock everyone was downstairs in a red-carpeted room as large as the one upstairs. The room was sensually lighted with colored lights. A mini light show was projected over a water bed in the middle of the room. People were making love in front of the fireplace and in a cozy area off the main room replete with wall-to-wall mattresses. At Sandstone there was none of the franticness that is so often the case of "swinging" parties. It seemed as though those who had sex just sort of flowed together rather than playing a lot of pursuer/pursued games. Throughout the evening, people scurried nude in the chill night air from the main building to the nearby housed-in swimming pool. I joined them. It was a very sensual experience, swimming and floating in the body-temperature water, hugging and laughing with the other nude people.

Everyone who attends these parties is invited to spend the night. I bedded down on the velvet couch while Pam slept on the thick, lush carpet with other weekenders.

I got up at 9:00 a.m., poured myself a cup of coffee, and went outside on the balcony. There I was, nude in the warm sunshine, overlooking the green hills and the not-so-far-away fogged-in ocean. Some people were already sunbathing on the lawn, while others were still wrapped in their sleeping bags. Still others rummaged in the kitchen, preparing an informal breakfast.

During the day a number of couples came and went, sunbathing, swimming, playing volley ball, hiking in the miles of surrounding hills, or just socializing and enjoying the freedom for intimacy fostered by the Sandstone environment. Toward dusk, the group began to trickle away down the hill to the distant glow of the city, ending another pleasant weekend.

Sandstone is run by several couples who live on the grounds and act as caretakers and coordinators. They share a philosophy of joyful living with their diversified membership. "The couples who have joined us have a common desire for honesty, acceptance, and freedom from artificiality," Barbara Williamson told me. "The Sandstone community believes that the human body is good and that open expressions of affection and sexuality are good." Their members include doctors, factory workers, actors and actresses, accountants, rock star, singers, nurses, students, business executives, lawyers, artists, explorers, teachers, et al. New applicants are interviewed personally and screened for compatibility with the Sandstone community. The membership fee is $100 per year and dues are $15 per month—or a $240.00 flat rate yearly.

The grounds, house, and cottages are open to members every day of the week except Monday, which is cleanup and recuperation day. About two hundred people come to Sandstone every weekend. Membership presently stands at two hundred- seventy- five couples with a projected four hundred by this summer. Singles may use the facilities daily, but the policy is couples only after 7:00 p.m. and on weekends.

The whole experience at Sandstone was free from the pressure, uneasiness, and bad vibrations one often gets from the "real" world. But for me personally, it lacked a certain spark, the excitement of activity, of people doing things. It was almost too mellow and relaxed—if that's possible.

The grapevine at Sandstone says there may be planned activities in the future: encounter groups, massage classes, dance parties, crafts, etc. This sounds like a good idea to me and to others who like to be active and involved. But then again, perhaps Sandstone should remain a retreat from programmed existence, a place to go where you can just BE.

Barbara Williamson told me, "The strength and lasting significance of the Sandstone experience lies in human contact divorced from the cocktail-party context with all its games and dodges and places to hide. Contact at Sandstone includes the basic level of literal, physical nakedness and open sexuality. In these terms, the experience goes far beyond any attempt to intellectualize it."

To this, I say, "Amen."

It was really terrific to meet and make welcome Margo and Pam. They were Sandstone's first lesbian couple. You must remember this was in the late sixties or early seventies; gay men were just beginning to make protests (albeit weakly) about civil rights. And gay women—well, they were still relegated to positions as gym teachers, spinster librarians, or someone's never-married maiden aunt who adopted stray cats. Luckily enough for me, Sandstone had always had its share of bisexual women, but Margo and Pam were the first truly committed couple. They had found a way to bond and accept and just *be*.

You know, in retrospect, I suddenly realize that we didn't have any gay male couples—or anyone who claimed to be homosexual. And I don't recall ever seeing any man-on-man sex at Sandstone. Now that I think about it, I find that very odd, because of course they would have been as welcome as anyone else. If any of our members or guests did have leanings toward homosexuality, I suppose they were too afraid of being exposed to others in the "real" world. Gays were often beaten up, fired from their jobs, turned away by their own families, and driven out of their communities if their sexuality was discovered. We've come a long, long way since then, and to that I say a hearty "Thank God!"

The Age of Aquarius did bring about a lot of changes. When we first opened Sandstone in the late sixties, it was met by shocked outrage and quickly dismissed as a "nudist camp" or just another "fuck club," a place of depravity that would ruin future generations. Very slowly, the tide turned in our favor. The same publications that had scorned our very existence were open-minded enough to check us out more closely before denouncing us. That's why I always said yes when any publication or TV show asked for an interview: I knew if they spent any time at all at Sandstone they would clearly see what we were all about. One of our most surprising supporters was *The Los Angeles Times,* a well-established, highly respected newspaper that had been around since the early 1900s. When talk of Sandstone first began to intrigue people, *The Times* wrote a short account of "just another hippie commune where members experiment with psychedelic drugs, tie-dye their clothing and grow their own marijuana"—which couldn't have been further from the truth. While it was true that in that era dozens of hippie communes had sprung up clear across the United States, none of them could have been considered homes like Sandstone. Consisting mostly of very young, restless, rootless kids just searching for a space they could call their own, they soon fell apart and were all gone by the midseventies.

On April 6, 1972, *The Los Angeles Times* ran an article titled "Sandstone: Close-up of a Unique Life-Style" by Staff Writer Skip Ferderber. It was probably the fairest and most concise article written about us at that time.

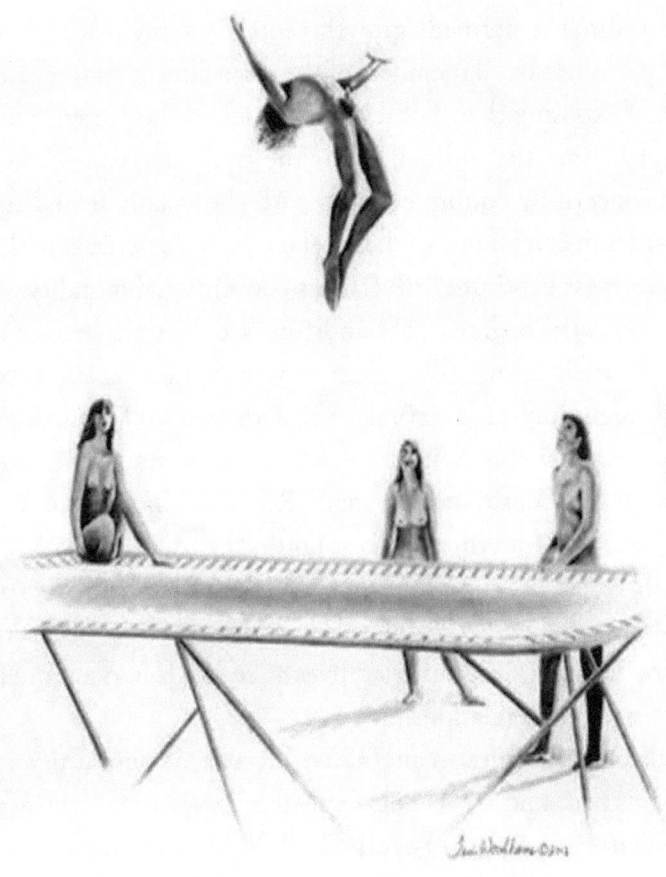

Let Freedom Ring

Although it was not probably intended, a recent State Court ruling had opened the way for a unique community and lifestyle to continue its highly controversial experimentation with relationships between men and women.

On the surface, the decision of the State Court of Appeals seemed mild enough. The judges struck down a County Ordinance requiring the licensing and regulation of "growth centers" (nudist camps), calling the ordinance "vague and overbroad" and in violation of the First Amendment of the Constitution, which guarantees the right to assembly.

Specifically, the measure endangered two Topanga Canyon centers: Elysium Fields and Sandstone Foundation. Both had been threatened with closure for operating without a county license.

The ordinance defined "growth centers" as any place where three or more persons, not all members of the same family, congregate for the purpose of exposing their bodies in the nude in the presence of others.

What neither the ordinance nor the court decision made explicit was the concern by county officials with the openly sexual nature of the activities in at least one of these centers, which, while kept discreetly away from mass exposure, still flaunts conventional morality.

Certainly, the operators of Sandstone see the decision as a de facto victory for their admittedly unusual way of life, which encourages relations beginning on a sexual level with two and sometimes three or more persons. But Sandstone, or more formally the Sandstone Foundation for Community Systems Research, Inc., is not a sex club or wife-swapping fraternity, at least not in the usual sense.

While there is a definite sexual basis for their interpersonal relationships, and while they may cross the formal lines of marriage, its proprietors see their intermingled lives as research into a more realistic approach to human relationships.

Sandstone combines an alternative lifestyle, a community, a private club and retreat, and a sociology research community, say its owners. Its headquarters is at 21400 Saddle Peak Road, a cluster of neatly kept buildings on a plush 15-acre hilltop site in the Malibu hills with a magnificent unobstructed view of the ocean.

At first glance, it resembles any number of well-kept homes in the hills: a $500,000.00 estate complete with a two-story ranch style house, guest cottages, covered swimming pool, a large green lawn, one quarter-mile back from the road and accessible only by driving down a pitted dirt road. The resemblance ends, however, when a visitor spots a well-tanned man and woman cleaning out the circulating fountain in front of the main house. Both are nude.

Relaxing inside in a spacious wood-lined living room with thick beige carpets are some of Sandstone's 14 permanent residents, some clothed, some not.

The building reflects the foundation's free and easy lifestyle. The administrative and play centers for the club, which lists some 500 members, the building is carpeted throughout, with furniture on the ground floor, and with mats or waterbeds on the lower floors. All the doors are open. Men and women are sitting and talking, some touching in a frank, sensual way, yet there is no sense of licentiousness. On the contrary, the atmosphere is relaxed and tension free.

Sandstone's founder, 39-year-old John Williamson, is soft-spoken, a slightly balding, rough-hewn man with a reserved, almost courtly manner. He discusses Sandstone's lifestyle and objectives which, he said, includes research into living in pluralistic (two, three or more people) relationships. "We believe in the sexual self as being the core of organized social behavior," he said. "When sexuality is distorted, it leads to a distortion of the basic self."

By Sandstone's mores, an individual may do what he desires providing the others, singly or together, are willing to go along. As a result, in one room of their retreat, people may be talking, playing chess, or engaging in sexual intercourse without any discrimination as to what is "proper."

Sandstone's financial life-blood comes from its club members, who pay $240 a year membership, allowing them to use the facilities whenever they desire. Wednesdays and Saturdays are party nights.

Couples only come to the retreat in the daytime to sunbathe, nude if desired, swim in the covered pool, read, play chess, and relax. At night, the downstairs is softly lighted. Softly swinging rock music plays. Couples are sitting and talking or sexually engaged, not necessarily with the partner they came with.

Some couples remain clothed. Most do not. It is neither obligatory to remove one's clothing or engage in any of the activities. On a full night, there are as many as 80 adult visitors to the retreat, of all races, ages, and backgrounds, both married and unmarried.

While newcomers may be awed by the open sexuality, most old timers are more relaxed by the atmosphere and say they thrive in an environment which allows them to experience without guilt or social stigma.

Sexuality, Williamson believes, can be a barrier to improving relationships but at the same time is irrelevant to their ultimate success or failure. For example, a man or woman may have emotional feelings for a co-worker, but because of social, moral, and legal boundaries, each is unable to form closer relationships with the other. Once the sexual barrier is gone, in Sandstone's view, a more fulfilling relationship is possible.

"We believe in the acceptance of the physical as well as the mental side of man's nature," said Martin Zitter, 29, director and public-relations man for Sandstone.

This freedom has a profound effect on marriages. But Sandstone devotees believe that a relationship can thrive by sharing individuals who bring pleasure of both a social and physical nature. "If the key to a relationship is based on a neurotic impulse," Williamson commented, "if they've captured each other, then they live in fear. In a healthy relationship, this will not happen. They understand the true nature of their contract."

With the traditional barrier or sexual fidelity no longer a factor, Sandstone residents claim their brand of relationships can create more meaningful human contacts.

The possibility of rejection becomes a more potent threat at the same time. But they believe a relationship which includes others while maintaining one primary relationship causes an incredibly strong bond to emerge. Thus, the individual's responsibility for creating a better relationship becomes far greater at Sandstone than in most other situations, they believe. It is up to each person to decide whether he desires to remain with one partner, as in marriage, or to have short-term relationships. While the first reaction of a newcomer to the community is usually one of heightened sexual appetite, it tends to diminish, and the individual becomes more selective.

"In addition," said filmmaker Jonathan Dana, 26, who lives at Sandstone with his wife, Bunny, 25, "this place is much less 'sexual' than any city I've ever lived in. There's no teasing, no exploitation, and no frustration." While to some palates this might seem paradise, all is not easy in Utopia. One couple, residents for eight months, is leaving. The feeling of the community is that the husband, a mechanic, "related better to machines than to people." The wife of one of the executives, in addition to living in the community for a short time, became involved with another man and left the community.

Ultimately, the members agree, the same emotions which exist in relations outside Sandstone exist inside Sandstone. "In practice," said Williamson, "we have all the differences that other people have, but as a community we are honest about it."

Those relationships tend to overlap and to become highly complicated. There are currently, among the permanent residents, two multiple relationships, one of a man and two women, the other of two men and one woman. In one case, one of the women is married. Her husband, who also lives at Sandstone, approves of his wife's participation in the ménage-à-trois.

The state court's action ends a two-year fight for the community, which claims it has spent $10,000.00 on legal fees fighting the county ordinance. While community members say they have no opposition from sheriffs' officers or from neighbors (the nearest is two miles away), protests from the Topanga Chamber of Commerce and some local residents were lodged with the county Public Welfare Commission, which denied them the county license in 1970 on the grounds it was a "detriment to the public welfare." According to residents, none of their opponents ever visited Sandstone.

The community's beginnings are based on the philosophical idols of Williamson and his outspoken wife, Barbara. Alabama-born John Williamson, an engineer by training, is a former project manager with Lockheed Aircraft who worked on design and management of missile support systems, including development of the Polaris missile. In the early 1960s, he opened his own electronics company then sold it to buy Sandstone in 1968. Barbara Williamson, 32, is a former insurance saleswoman.

Williamson's belief is in "nonstructured experiential processes, which contribute significantly to the release and actualization of positive human potential." Simply put, do your own thing to the fullest and enjoy the process. In addition to being an experimental community, some of the residents also say they consult with various organizations on developing a community process within business, religious organizations, and at least one private psychological clinic.

According to Williamson, their outside work helps organizations look upon their employees and management as a community, and Sandstone people are available to help them develop a community sense in their business—but without the sexual overtones. How much applicability Sandstone has to the outside world is debatable, but Williamson believes the community's message is important, serving to point up the true if unconventional nature of people. He also believes it is not for everybody.

"But," he said, "we should be able to accept alternatives within our social structures. Society is too complex to support only one lifestyle. All of our lives are changing." Sandstone, he added, is not looking for people to live on the property. "We're looking for people to become individuals through Sandstone. You don't have to live here to get what you need."

Chapter 9

FOR THE FIRST FOUR DECADES after its inception, no one ever asked why we created what came to be known as Sandstone Retreat. Finally, an astute documentary maker and producer of the History Channel posed the question. What a relief! The big question did reveal some interesting aspects and shortcomings of human nature. We showered them with documents that amply illustrated that Sandstone was not a sex club as most outsiders thought but a very differently managed project. It was a retreat that would give people the opportunity to experience something different. It was an environment that would help people to reconnect with nature and then with their own latent natural values.

While John and I were looking for deeper meaning, it seemed that no one—reporters, writers, TV producers, or even members themselves—could get past the breathtaking beauty and richness of Sandstone. So I asked John, "Why do you think every article written about us raved about our house and furnishings and the surrounding grounds?"

"Because," he said, "it was a Shangri-la sort of setting. The fifteen acres of rugged, wildly beautiful forest, a box canyon almost at the top of a three - thousand-foot mountain range made it all seem surreal.

It was funnel-shaped, and the mouth of the funnel ended abruptly at the edge of a sheer drop of several hundred feet. This tended to focus perception over a panorama of receding hills toward the ocean and beyond to distant islands. We were completely surrounded on three sides by rising cliffs and countless trees. It was quiet and isolated. You could be anywhere in this natural, womb-like setting and look out and down over a tranquil world of earth, sky, and water with no abrupt discontinuity. You became a part of it. It clasped you and held you to its values, its perspective."

I nodded in agreement, remembering how, no matter how many thousands of times I beheld the sight of my surroundings, there was always a little intake of breath at the splendor of it all. John and I were sitting in the living room of our home in Fallon, Nevada, talking about the writing of this book. I had already spoken with several members from the old days and had gone through thousands of pages of material that had been published about Sandstone, but I had never really sat down with John and asked him about his memories.

"You know, it's kind of interesting that every article ever written about Sandstone went on and on about the house, about how luxurious it was."

"It was plush," John said, "but not ostentatious or dominating in any way. It was extremely comfortable and subdued. We wanted it to be homelike, anti-institutional. We created a lot of nooks and crannies and natural grouping areas, which were filled with books and plants and other ordinary things. We brought soft form chairs and cut the legs off so you were forced into a relaxed sprawl. The couches, as well, were soft and inviting.

"As a bit of incongruity, we had a pool table at one end of the ballroom. That kept the whole works from flying out in space. All in all, the downstairs space was designed to reflect, intensify, and bring a sharp awareness of prevailing sexual attitudes within our culture. The upstairs enhanced the alternative. The total experience gave one a good sense of the yin and yang of things. It was just an automated takeoff on some of Jung's primal symbolism. It was a not-so-gentle reminder of where one stood and where one could go."

We made sure there would be no withdrawal into some sort of structural privacy by removing all the doors in the house (with the exception of the outside doors, of course), so the result was that a central bathroom opened up right in the middle of a main traffic pattern and was continually used for passage from one area to another. A woman who conducted anthropological studies for UCLA and who frequented Sandstone came up with a metaphor that best describes the environmental impact of the retreat. Her paper describes our lives as conducted either "on stage" or "backstage." In view of others, we lead stage lives, role-playing with masks and costumes that are designed to create certain images of ourselves. Only in privacy, backstage, do we dare remove our masks and costumes, be natural, and be ourselves. Few of us allow the outside world to view our backstage behavior. I remembered when I invited Berry Gordy to remove his clothes and get comfortable. His reply: "Oh no. If I take off my clothes, no one will know who I am!"

There was no backstage at Sandstone. Whatever anyone did was done openly in front of everyone else. I always felt that constant exposure made it virtually impossible to be dishonest. At first, guests and members did try to seek a sort of retreat for themselves, but they quickly realized there was no place to hide. Eventually they just gave in and happily discovered that complete honesty felt better. That, of course, was our goal at Sandstone. To further aid in bringing down barriers and defenses, there was our magnificent Olympic-sized swimming pool.

"Keeping the temperature at 93 degrees was crucial," John said. "There's a balanced heat flow between the water and the body, so you end up not being able to feel the water. It's a mild form of sensory deprivation. It takes your focus off the external environment and puts you in your head without any distractions. And swimming is a good way to get used to nudity, a good excuse to take off your knickers. When suburban neighborhood friends go down to the beach and say,

'Let's go skinny dipping,' they really just want to see each other naked and probably want to go to bed with each other. That's a sneaky but acceptable way to peek at cocks and cunts—which their 'sensible' upbringing denies them. Our pool was a great place for hugging and kissing but terrible for fucking, although people tried because of the novelty of it."

A lot of people still thought that Sandstone was just a "fuck club," even after hundreds of magazine articles and dozens of television interviews, but the members who approached their time at Sandstone as a turning point in their lives were the only reward John and I needed. There were countless professionals and social scientists who visited us for the interesting experiment we offered. Like I said, our doors were always open—all you had to do was walk through. Actually, we did try to keep our membership at a manageable number, but as I look back through our records and files I see (somewhat to my amazement) that we entertained about eight thousand people during the five years we were open. There's no doubt we could have turned Sandstone into a huge money-making venture, but it would have meant giving up our values and turning our lovely home into the aforementioned fuck club. That just wasn't going to happen.

According to my records, each year we had about five hundred memberships, 75 percent from professional classes, 90 percent upper-middle class, 5 percent that could be considered extremely wealthy, 5 percent blue-collar, 5 percent hippie, 7 percent black, and 3 percent Asian or Hispanic. I think that's a pretty healthy cross-section of America. After they were screened and accepted, we told them, "Sandstone is a place where you can do what you want to do. We give you permission. We don't wear clothes, but you don't have to take yours off unless you want to. We fuck a lot in front of other people, but you don't have to unless you want to. We've taken away all the no-nos of life—so the only ones left are in your own head."

Having told all our guests the rules (there weren't any, really) they were on their own. They could use the place as merely a swing club, or as a country club with full use of all the facilities, or as a mechanism for a deeper understanding of themselves—a mechanism for change. The choice was theirs.

"You know, pumpkin," John said. "We really did try to keep everything normal, and I think we did, for the most part. Parties around the clock were just too much for anyone, but a party on Saturday night was perfectly normal. Isn't that when straight people go to parties?"

"That's true," I laughed, "but the big difference between a Sandstone party and a so-called normal party is nudity. When someone walked through our door, everyone was naked and open sexuality was permitted, but everything else was the same—good food, good wine, great music, interesting people, fascinating conversation."

"Yeah—and a lot more fucking on Saturday nights. It could range from a wild orgy-type thing to everybody sitting around playing chess or intellectualizing. There was an awful lot of that. The fucking was there—it was a given—so it wasn't all that important anymore."

"It was to the newcomers," I said. "Fucking was like being let loose in a candy store for the first time."

"At first, sure. They'd get off on all the fantasies and think, 'My God, is this really happening?' and that would probably last a couple of weeks, but to the people who had been around for a while, the fucking was there if they felt like it; if not, it didn't make any difference. People soon realized no matter how exciting it was and how good it felt, a person simply cannot fuck twenty- four hours a day."

"And that's when the bonding began," I said. "I think that's the part I loved the most, everyone sitting around together, having a cocktail or glass of wine, sharing their thoughts and emotions, completely satiated. Women were on equal ground with men, and both voices were equally heard."

"I've always said it's a woman's world. Especially at Sandstone—no chauvinists allowed. I think that might have scared some of the guys when they realized that women just wanted intimacy."

That is a word I want to emphasize. There was a lot of intimacy at Sandstone—and it was the most difficult aspect for anyone to cope with. That's why we insisted on having couples who wanted to work on their relationships, not just a bunch of horny single guys who were there to see how many women they could bed. Couples who were serious about their relationships would spend a month or two attending parties, bonding with other couples, learning about each other. Then they would go off and internalize their experiences. They realized they had changed, and now they had to bring those changes into their everyday lives.

In essence, they would discover that they were two new people who would have to go through courtship all over again. When they came back to Sandstone for, let's say, one of the big Saturday-night parties, they realized it was no longer just about sex. There was an awareness and a new closeness. The man would tend to lose his chauvinism and become more sensitive, more oriented toward giving pleasure. People at Sandstone learned to confront their fears; then getting rid of them was relatively simple. The environment was designed with this in mind. Sandstone was certainly a fun place to hang out, even though you would be dealing with serious issues.

"The most common fears were the old American standbys," John said. "The men were worried about the size of their cock, and the women were worried about the shape of their breasts. That may sound trivial, but under psychiatric analysis, these fears always surface. A predominant male fear was the fear of homosexuality. Men didn't want to see another man naked. They were afraid another guy might turn them on; but for women, this was exciting. They wanted to see another nude female body. Also, men were afraid of losing affection. This comes from the old ownership thing. 'What if another guy is a better lover and my wife or girlfriend leaves me for him?' There were always performance fears with new guests—especially the men. Men were always in competition. They weren't so much worried about satisfying a woman but in being measured against other men. They were afraid every other man in the room was judging them, checking out their technique while comparing the size of their erection. After a couple of visits they realized none of that silly shit meant anything, and their self-esteem went through the roof. They were accepted with open arms; they were caressed, held close, and deeply satisfied. They could lie next to another naked man, equally satisfied, with no fear of ridicule or rejection. That's when the true meaning of intimacy became clear in their minds."

In the beginning we did have a problem with swingers wanting to hang out at Sandstone and just have sex with as many partners as they could. Swingers are always attracted to a new place to fuck, but the environment at Sandstone simply wouldn't allow that. It forced an intimacy they couldn't handle, and they would just sort of fade away.

Another type that I immediately kicked to the curb was the creepy voyeurs. They set themselves apart as if they were above everything and better than the rest of us. It was just a pathetic way of covering up their prurient interests. I suppose they felt if they weren't actually participating in intercourse (just sitting in a dark corner masturbating) they somehow were keeping themselves pure. I do not tolerate hypocrites.

From the beginning of our experiment at Sandstone, John and I regularly examined and reassessed our own relationship. To my surprise, but not to John's, we discovered it had solidified.

"That's because we are very happy and comfortable with each other," John said. "The values into which we have changed have made for a tremendous relationship between us. It is certainly beyond anything we had ever hoped for based on our previous experience. And according to people with whom we talk, it's beyond anything they have ever seen."

There are very few people who do not want what we have. We try to explain to them that this is the result of very hard work. And some of them, even though they see the results in us, cannot see themselves walking down this path of commitment. But one day, if they dare to get involved in their own changes, they will know from their own experience how we got to where we are now. I have to admit, it was much harder for me in the beginning. When John had sex with another woman, I was consumed with jealousy—a hard, painful, frightening jealousy. I was overwhelmed with a desperate feeling of possessiveness, terrified that I would lose the object of my satisfaction. John was my husband, my love, and I wanted him all to myself. I was afraid to share him for fear I would lose him. I thought my jealousy was a measure of my deep love for him.

"Jealousy as an emotion does not really exist," John said. "It's a very complex behavioral response to fear of loss. All of our explorations lead to this single conclusion. Jealousy is a conditioned, learned response to a simple situation, which is rooted in fear. Jealousy is indicative of a castrating personality. Someone who treats another person as an object which can be bought, sold, won, or lost."

For at least a full year after John and I were married, I struggled with my own personal demons. I listened to every word he said and would find myself swept away by his deep baritone; the soothing, melodic, sensual sound of his voice was hypnotic, but that made me even more jealous. I didn't want any other woman to hear those words spoken just to her. When John was speaking to a group of people, I had no problem, even though I could see that the women in the group were gazing up at him with desire, as moved as I was by the sound of his voice. But I was okay with that, because I was the one sitting by his side. It was only when he went off with another woman that the old green-eyed monster reared its ugly head. I would suddenly be filled with a craving to be with him. I felt a real loss, because he was sharing his time, himself, with someone else.

"I refer to that as time jealousy, and it is indeed a real emotion," John said. "There is actually a solution. If your unit or group is cohesive and living in the same space, there is no need for time jealousy. You are all together; you share. It comes into play only when there is a relationship outside the core unit and time is spent apart from each other."

I admit that is something I had to work on and deal with on a daily basis. John knew this was something I had to ease into, so we decided to minimize its occurrence as much as possible. If John was with someone too long and I began to experience time jealousy, I would send him a signal. And he would be considerate enough to come back to me, often bringing the other woman with him.

"Our solution was not to go away from each other. If we want to be with someone, let it be with both of us. This way there is no chance for time jealousy, because we all share and are a part of it."

The ability to really love begins with being able to love yourself, to accept yourself for whatever you are. If you don't love yourself, you cannot love someone else. As I mentioned earlier in this book, that was always my main problem. The way I was raised had emotionally crippled me. I was just a little girl who wanted to be loved, to be held and comforted, to be understood and accepted, but these needs were met with coldness and rejection. If my own kin didn't love me, how could I expect anyone else to love me? How could I love myself? When I met John, it was like a lifeline being thrown to a drowning person. I grabbed ahold and held on, thinking, hoping his love would make up for the deficiencies I saw in myself. If I could just hold onto him, keep him in a cage of sorts for my own exclusive needs, I would be fulfilled and safe. It took me a while to realize that isn't what love is all about. You have to love and respect yourself first so you can then extend those feelings to others. When you are in touch with yourself, whole and complete, you don't need anyone else to fill the void in yourself. When I discovered I was bisexual and embraced it without embarrassment or fear, when I was able to treat my lovers with respect and acceptance, I truly felt complete.

"That's because you and I were so comfortable in our love for one another, pumpkin, that we found it easy to love other people. We found that living that lifestyle filled us both with more love. There was no loss, only gain. Thinking that open sexuality creates promiscuity is complete fantasy. It actually reduces promiscuity. Sexual sharing increases the bonds of friendship. Our marriage became more intense, more fulfilling. The satellites are those parts of the two people that are not fulfilled by each other but are fulfilled by relationships with other people. I can't tell you the deep, overwhelming love I always felt for you when I saw you reach climax with another woman. You were experiencing a feeling that I knew you loved, and I loved it for you. You were never more beautiful than you were at those times, and I was never more deeply in love. How could I be jealous of anything (or anyone) that brought you such enormous pleasure? Since Western society places so much importance on the longevity of marriage—the longer you're married, the happier and more in love you are—then I would say our marriage gets a big old gold star, wouldn't you?"

Over four decades together, moving up to a half a century—not bad! Of course, we were also living in a time that was conducive to experimentation. The sixties was a perfect decade for exploration and change. Sandstone would have been impossible in the staid fifties. It was most certainly the sexual revolution of the younger generation, the Age of Aquarius, that had a great deal to do with the receptiveness to new ideas. Also, the pill was a revelation to women. For the first time in history, there was birth control for women that was viable, available, and safe. No longer were we held prisoner by the fear of unwanted pregnancy. A general relaxation of the old prohibitive values allowed experimentation to take place. John always told prospective members that sexuality is the core factor in determining whether a society will behave sanely and further its potential or insanely and thus bring about its own destruction or diminishment. Repression of sexuality promotes violence, retardation, and distortion of psychological growth. Repression makes for a confused identity both in individuals and in society.

And the more confusion there is about one's identity, the more insecure, ego dependent, and ungrounded one becomes—separated, so to speak, from the genetic wisdom of ecological processes. Although the sexual freedom of the younger generation was labeled as mere rebellion, it did touch a nerve that hastened the discovery of real issues.

"They were calling it the youth movement in the beginning of the teenage rumblings; then, about mid to late sixties, it was the hippie generation. The kids were protesting racism, Vietnam, Nixon, ecology, sexual repression, et cetera. They really couldn't do a damn thing about the politics or government, but they did have complete control over their bodies and their sexuality, so they joined hands and marched boldly into the sexual revolution. As a society, we harassed our children, set them apart, spied on them, and even killed them in a frenzy of psychotic reaction to their clear perception of affairs. The older generation was horrified by the open sexuality of its youth. When communes began to spring up which embraced group living and sharing and the casual exchange of sexual partners, the bulk of our good Christian population believed they were going straight to hell. If they had taken a minute to do a little research, they would have discovered that there are cultures in the world where this kind of behavior is openly condoned, even institutionalized. There are cultures in which group marriage or communal forms of sexuality are absolutely permissible. Even if they are not the norm, they exist as an alternative within the social structure and as a bonding element. The end product is synergy—and peace, since these lifestyles give little reason to fight."

Acceptance depends entirely on change, but the establishment or older generation was rigid and unyielding. Real change occurs within us and results in growth and maturity; it is the very essence of life. The lack of change results in stagnation and eventually death. Everything in life is going to keep on changing whether we like it or not, so wouldn't it be smarter to change with the times? That's what we offered at Sandstone: a chance to change attitudes, to bond and work in unison. Dropping the puritanical approach to sex is the first and most important change we can make. Every time we interviewed a new member or whenever John was just talking to some of the casual guests, he stressed the importance of keeping an open mind, being willing to accept a new concept.

"We need to recognize change for what it is," John told them. "It's a fundamental break with old values and assumptions which have regulated our daily behavior and the way in which we relate to others and to society. This kind of change can take place in deep and profound ways both in individuals and society, if only they are given the appropriate structure and mechanisms to accomplish it. So far, we have not looked in the right direction for these mechanisms. We have not allowed ourselves to take advantage of the available tools or motivation in order to reach transcendence.

"Instead, we have given ourselves incredible weapons, divisive religions, overly packed cities, Barbie dolls, and questionable politics. We have a worldwide arsenal of weapons in the hands of a few individuals who are predominately psychopathic. We have a stupid situation of a two-thousand- times overkill capacity of nuclear weapons. Not to mention all the mutated viruses and other clever packages of mass death. Our technology is so good that an average college student can make the same weapons in a well- equipped kitchen. At the same time, we have not produced any compensating technology of sanity and emotional balance.

"So, without further elaboration, as a society and as a species we are facing very bad times as a result of our own doing. But we are also very close to the nexus. After much suffering and bloodshed, for the first time in recorded history, we have the technology and sheer operational knowledge so that we could choose our own destiny from here on out. Mother Nature has finally given us the ball and figures we're old enough to play the game on our own. Just don't try to foist off any plastic or margarine on her!

"Our problems do have solutions if we stop playing with the symptoms and look at their core. We can keep our technological base, our marvelously materialistic style, and get in balance with our ecology. We need to do a dance with Dionysius, to drop our love affair with Aristotle, the aging whore, and take up with Whitehead, practically a virgin.

"My interest now is very much global. I am concerned with a global economy, a global ecology—with where we are going in the next hundred years. We need people who can arrive at complex answers to very complex problems by virtue of having different bodies of knowledge. One sets out to be a human being. You learn all you can about the world you live in to improve yourself. It's different from setting out to be a doctor, attorney, engineer, or whatever. For instance, a total grasp of architecture is not going to solve the city's problems. A total grasp of psychology is not, nor a total grasp of economics. But a single mind or a group of different minds can operate in such a manner that they infuse each other with these different fields of knowledge. Then you might begin to see some answers, because you will see the whole problem, not just little, narrow parts of it.

"This is what now concerns me—how to bring more of this knowledge and unity about. It's a natural outgrowth of Sandstone, because some of the same mechanisms and the same dynamics that we now know so well can be applied here."

As I'm writing these words now, John's words, I can close my eyes and see him sitting in one of the low-slung chairs in the living room at Sandstone, surrounded by a group of admiring, adoring members and guests. His deep, melodious baritone caressed the senses. He was so soft-spoken and low-key that people had to lean forward to hear him. More than once, a guest approached me and excitedly whispered, "Gosh, Barb, he's like this ethereal guru, isn't he? I could just listen to him forever."

Through the years I often wondered why people were so drawn to John. His physical appearance was unassuming, pleasant more than arresting, and his demeanor was mild-mannered and unthreatening. And yet he was like the proverbial pied piper, the flame that moths could not resist. His voice was so rich and full, so mellifluous it flowed over you like warm honey. Every woman who came to Sandstone quickly fell under his spell, and the fact that he was completely devoted to me was a huge turn-on for them. There were very few people who did not want what we had. I must have heard this statement hundreds of times: "Wow, Barbara, you are so lucky. What I wouldn't do to have a marriage like you guys have!"

I always tried to explain that our marriage was the result of hard work. There had been a lot of kinks to work through, and a lot of changes had to be made for both of us to live a life of commitment to one another. The biggest obstacle, of course, was jealousy on my part. It was really difficult to know that the man I loved so deeply was also loved and desired by dozens of other women. People often asked us how it was possible to love more than one person. It was a classic question and usually asked in a tone that implied that sharing our love among many was somewhat of an insult to the concept of true love, but we saw it differently. If you truly love someone, nothing brings you greater joy than to see that person happy. When I finally embraced my bisexuality and brought other women into our relationship, John was just as happy as I was, saying, "To see my wife, the woman I love, feeling such pleasure fills me with joy. We are very happy and comfortable with each other. The values into which we have changed have made for a tremendous relationship between us. It certainly is beyond anything we had ever hoped for based on our previous experience. And according to people we talk to, it's beyond anything they've ever seen."

Obviously, all of us have felt many kinds of love in our lives—the love of parents, children, good friends, pets, and so on—but that's a different kind of love, right? But what makes it different? The obvious answer has to be sex. John and I brought outside sex into our marriage and found it made our marriage stronger.

To the others living at Sandstone with us (the family), I'm sure it must have seemed like John and I had all the answers. We were the model for a perfect marriage. But in reality, we were working on our relationship every day. There was a big difference between coming to Sandstone as a guest and actually living there. With that many people sharing the same space, there were the inevitable politics and intrigues. That's why we closed the doors on Monday and spent that time discussing our problems and concerns as well as recuperating from the steady stream of visitors and nonstop partying. It's kind of funny, but the main problem everyone had was the same problem that normal families have: Who does the chores? Who cleans up the mess after a party of fifty or sixty people?

Tom Hatfield, a writer who had been living with us for several months, spoke for everyone when he said, "You know, most of the guests who come up for weekends treat us like servants. They leave their trash lying around, they never pick up their towels or wash their own dishes—nothing, man."

"They don't even carry their dishes into the kitchen and put them in the sink," Sue said. "They just leave them for us to pick up, because they know we will."

"Well, we have to, don't we?" Marty shrugged. "I mean, it's our home, and we take pride in it and want to keep it looking nice." "You guys have a valid point," I said, "but let's be fair. There are quite a few members who do pitch in and help clean up before they go home. We just need to stress to all our members that they are expected to clean up after themselves, put their towels in the hamper, wash their own dishes, empty their ashtrays—just as if Sandstone was their own home. As for the family, well, let's write up a chore list and give everyone their own job like vacuuming, laundry, grocery shopping, cooking, cleaning the kitchen, yard work, pool maintenance, keeping the books. We can all choose the job we want so no one will be stuck doing something they don't like."

Since John's background was engineering, he handled the maintenance of the machinery. He was also probably the only one who wasn't afraid to drive the bulldozer, so he kept the roads graded and free of debris. We kind of figured out the chores on the level of competency—who was the most competent to handle a particular task. Tom's background was in graphics and publishing, so it fell to him to handle the newsletter and any new literature we might generate. He also planned special events and any other projects that would benefit Sandstone.

Marty had been managing the place ever since we opened, but his strength was really in public relations, and he was great with people, so the reins of management went to Tom. My specialty was keeping the books, and I had a good system worked out. The finances were everyone's responsibility from the standpoint of getting receipts for purchases and keeping the desk log up-to-date and accurate, and I handled the overall bookkeeping chores. I also did a lot of the interviewing, and I was good at it. I approached it as a business, so I didn't take any shit; it was pretty much, "Okay, this is who we are, here's how much it costs, take it or leave it!" Marty was the people pleaser, so he wasn't quite as abrupt.

Sue's main tasks were taking care of the club's membership records, typing the monthly billing, and helping Marty with public relations. Janice loved being outdoors, and she spent most of her time watering the plants and flowers, sweeping the eucalyptus debris and dead leaves off the driveway, and so on. She would often pick huge bouquets of wildflowers and bring them inside to grace an end table and lend a touch of beauty. Summers in Topanga Canyon could be brutal, and watering everything was a full-time job.

For a while I only had one cat living with me. Pusso was a large, beautiful, all black Manx who let everyone know he was the real head of the household. Talk about attitude—he had it in spades! On party nights he celebrated by finding a female that he liked and snuggled up next to her on the sofa and sucked on all her fingers for hours. The years we lived there, many different cats would stop by and stay a while. I remember one cute little guy that Meg found living in one of the storm drains. It took her weeks to coax it out and convince it to become sociable with everyone. With my deep love for all felines, any time a stray wandered by, I automatically invited it to stay as long as it wanted to. At one point there were about fourteen cats living with us at Sandstone, and they had a variety of interesting names: PC, Mouse, Jasper, Gypsy, Ashley, Chin, the Professor, AC (Another Cat), DC (De Last Cat)—I'm sorry to say I can't remember all their names, but they were well loved and well treated for as long as they were with us. Some didn't last too long because of the natural predators that lived in the mountains.

One of the tasks that fell to Tom Hatfield as manager was working the door—greeting people when they first arrived at Sandstone, signing them in the register, checking their membership status, receiving dues or guest fees, and in the case of people coming for the first time, explaining what we were all about. Sounds pretty simple, right? Well, it wasn't, and no one liked working the door but Tom seemed to handle it better than most. He told me it was actually one of the more interesting functions associated with the club, and it provided him with a tremendous amount of fun, frustration, friends, and enemies. Most people didn't knock; they just walked right in. If we did hear a knock at the door, we knew it was someone who had never been there before.

One day we were all sitting around in the living room talking when we heard a knock. Tom opened the door, and there was a very straight-looking young man dressed in a black suit and tie and a crisp white shirt and what can only be described as an establishment haircut, very short. This was the early seventies, and everyone wore their hair long, some much longer than others. Everyone was nude, of course, and the young man just stood there, his mouth hanging open, clutching a copy of *The Watchtower* close to his chest almost like a shield. After an awkward silence, John invited the man inside, someone brought him a cup of coffee, and he sat perched on the edge of his chair while John engaged him in conversation about religion. When he left, we all collapsed into giggles, wondering what kind of story he would tell when he got back down the mountain. How he had managed to find his way up the treacherous little dirt road is beyond me!

Chapter 10

THE SUMMER OF 1971, JOHN and I received a letter from Jonathan and Bunny Dana asking if they could come to Sandstone and meet with us, as they were interested in doing a documentary about the work we were doing. During our meeting we discovered that they had a platonic living arrangement with Ron, who was also part of their film company. They all lived together in Palo Alto. Ron was along for the first meeting at Sandstone. As it turned out, Ron's primary interest was not focused on making a Sandstone movie. He met and fell hard for Meg, Marty's wife, which was a terrible interruption and injustice to the daily Sandstone lifestyle, particularly since Meg agreed to pack her bags and move to Palo Alto with Ron. Meg and Marty's relationship instantly disintegrated without any discussion between the two of them. And furthermore, Meg seemed unaware that she was important to John and me and the Sandstone community. Meg failed to give any of us an explanation of why she would just cast these known relationships aside in favor of someone she had known for only forty-eight hours. This left Bunny shaking her head and asking, "What the hell happened? We've only been here a few days, and both of the men I love are gone!" Since Ron did not have any regard for the Sandstone community, he was barred from living at Sandstone and working on the movie.

This was the start of the Sandstone movie.

Jonathan found his crash pad with Nancy until Bunny returned from Washington DC, where she was finishing a project on free clinics, and as soon as that film wrapped, she too moved into Sandstone. By that time we were filled to overflowing with live-in guests, but we were able to find space for Bunny and Jonathan in a small bedroom in the main house. John and I were still spending our nights with PC in our motor home so, that opened the main house up a bit more. I have to admit I really loved all the activity and all the happy, eager faces that greeted me each morning. Everyone was really excited about doing a movie. It was something different, and it was a lot of fun to be a part of the creativity of moviemaking.

None of the film crew had ever been to Sandstone before, so there was a lot of wide-eyed ogling the first few days. The crew consisted of about a dozen young, single men, and although they tried really hard to maintain a professional attitude, they were clearly overwhelmed by all the lovely naked females wandering about. Bunny had planned on a seven-week shooting schedule, and she managed to stick to the routine in spite of the casual, laid-back atmosphere of Sandstone. Sort of as a joke, Bunny started referring to John as the messiah of sex, and it stuck. Several times in future articles and interviews, reporters would begin, "John Williamson, the messiah of sex ..."

One thing about shooting the movie really irritated me, even though I knew it was only temporary—the numerous black cords and wires that were tangled all over the beautiful grounds. Huge tripods held large lights and other paraphernalia, their sharp legs digging into the lawn. Fortunately, it only took about a week of watering and raking to get everything back in order after the crew left. Several times when the crew was taking a break, I noticed a thick haze of smoke hanging in the air above them and smelled the sweet aroma of marijuana. I never saw where they discarded the roaches, but the next spring we discovered a few marijuana plants among the other foliage around the house where some errant seeds had taken root. It was a hardy little weed!

There were mixed feelings about whether the film honestly portrayed life at Sandstone. I liked it and enjoyed the whole process, but I was just as happy to see them leave.

By mid-September, John and I (and PC) had taken a couple of trips up north. I don't know if you could call it burnout or not, but we had been talking about starting a more large-scale community in a different part of the country. After four years of floods, fire, and earthquakes, our survivor skills had been sorely tested. We both liked the idea of settling on solid ground in the Pacific Northwest. We were also looking for a place where PC could have more freedom. I felt bad about him dividing his time between a motor home and a VW Bug. Every member and guest who passed through Sandstone had very strong opinions about PC, but I think Tom Hatfield explained it most succinctly in his book *Sandstone Experience:*

When PC was younger, we all thought he was a very pretty kitty-type bobcat, but as he grew older, we gained a great deal of respect for him. He was, without doubt, the most valid feedback we could get on where we were psychologically at a given time.

PC decided that the most interesting thing he could do on his frequent trips to the main house was to test us. How does a bobcat test? Well, he might just sit in front of you and stare. Now, having a bobcat sit and stare isn't my idea of the best way to start your day off, and since the early morning was when he was usually in the house, that's when most of the testing went on.

Not only would he sit and stare at you, but after a few minutes, he would lift his butt off the carpet and start wiggling it back and forth. Now I don't care if it's a bobcat or a regular little pussycat, when they start doing that it means they're getting ready to pounce! How do you feel about having a bobcat pounce on you? Well, we found out, because he would pounce. Actually, he wasn't jumping on you so much as jumping over you. It's just that he would kind of run up the front of you in the process of getting over the top. As long as you did nothing more than cover your eyes, there was little danger he would hurt you.

That is, unless he found out you were really afraid of him. Then it was a different story. He would drive you out of the house by just sitting on the back of the couch and staring at your ear.

One of his favorite games was to hide behind the couch and jump out at you when you came in from the kitchen. He did this to me once when I had a cup of coffee in my hand. Only he didn't jump past me, he jumped on me. All four paws on my naked front! Thank God he usually kept his claws in!

The force of his leap knocked some coffee out of my cup, and I had to stop a minute to get my balance. When PC hit the floor and turned to see what my reaction to his attack had been, he saw a sitting duck. Without even stopping to give me a second chance, he jumped again. Only this time only three paws were on me. The fourth one was taking a wild swing at that coffee cup. If I hadn't been knocked backward about one inch, he'd have had that coffee all over him and the carpet. John chased him away before he tried for strike three!

He played this particular game on me so often that it finally got a little boring. So, to stir things up, one morning I played a trick on him. He dodged behind the couch when I headed for the kitchen, and when I came out, I walked especially heavy. Then, just before I got to where he was going to jump, I stopped, but kept on stomping my feet. He fell for it. He leaped out a good two feet in front of me. When he landed without hitting anything, he turned around and gave me a look that could've killed. He walked away from me as I stood there laughing, but I knew it was only a temporary victory. You just don't laugh at a bobcat without expecting some repercussions.

He got his chance a couple of nights later. It was one of those quiet nights when nobody had come up, and John brought PC into the house. The phone rang, and I answered it. It was some guy asking for information about the club, so I started giving him the tape-recorded-type answers we usually give when all of sudden I had a twenty-pound bobcat sitting on my head with all four paws in my face!

"Hey, uh, I'm sorry, but I've got a bobcat sitting on my head." "What?"

"Please don't ask me to repeat. Could you call back tomorrow?" "I guess so. What's on your head?"

"Good night." Of course, PC jumped off as soon as I hung up the phone.

When I was going through a big emotional adjustment I couldn't go over to the house too early, because PC could sense the conflict and frustration in my behavior and just wouldn't leave me alone. The last thing I needed at that time was a bobcat psyching me out.

He seemed to have a special thing for the female members of the family, and I'd say he freaked out every one of them with the exception of Bunny. He was playing with her one evening and, almost by accident, bit her in the forearm. He knew he had goofed. He looked up at her and John with a very embarrassed expression in his eyes, but couldn't let go. John finally got his jaws apart.

Bunny wasn't the only person he bit. He bit Janice, too, but that was because she was scared of him—so scared she refused to come into the house when he was there, which was the smartest thing to do. There's no sense asking for trouble, especially from a bobcat, because he can give you plenty.

We were all curious about what PC would do to the other cats around the place, and he showed us. PC loved to play in the large fishpond in front of the house (he also loved to swim in the pool with John), and one afternoon he got out of the VW and walked up on the porch. Well, we had one cat, Jasper, who was a real city slicker. He'd just strut around the place totally fearless. He just happened to be on the porch that day, and when he saw PC he stopped long enough to see what this big dude would do.

Before Jasper had time to think, PC knocked him into the pond and then bounced him off the bottom about six times with his big paw. Jasper finally came out from under his paw and came out of the water with every hair on his body sticking straight out even though he was soaking wet. We saw another cat literally walking on water to get away from PC under similar circumstances.

He spent most of the day and evening in the VW parked out front the main house. John left the windows down several inches for air, and when PC would get tired of chewing the door and window knobs, his favorite stunt was to hide on the floor and wait for some unsuspecting person to walk by the car within his reach. Then he would come off the floor like a bullet, stick his paw straight out the window and smack the hapless passerby. One night he did it to a member who was headed for the pool, but instead of just smacking her, he grabbed her towel and took it back into the car. John had to go and talk him into giving it back.

If John and I made the mistake of not feeding him on time, he would take their sheets off the bed and shit right in the middle of their mattress! It kept them on schedule!

Gay Talese made the mistake of ignoring PC. Granted, it wasn't a good idea to stare at him, because he took that as a challenge, but it was even worse to ignore him. He finally stared Gay out of the house.

The last few months we were open, it was difficult for any of us to handle PC. We were all on edge, and he knew it. So it got to the point where John and I and PC pretty much had the house to ourselves in the morning. Finally we had to bring it up at a meeting and tell them we thought they were kind of laying their trip on us. They didn't really agree, but PC didn't come in so often.

The friendliest thing PC could do was turn around and present his balls to a person. To be allowed to rub a bobcat's balls was definitely an act of faith. Unfortunately, most of the people he would allow to rub his balls had no desire to do so, and they didn't even know what he wanted when he presented his butt to them. They thought he might be part skunk or something.

It was during the last week of filming the movie that PC ran away. It was a pure case of friction with John, and PC had to express his independence. That was a week when everything went wrong, so it was especially bad. John and I didn't hold out much hope for his return. There were lots of bobcats running wild and living in the hills around

Sandstone, so it was just assumed that PC had found a mate and set up housekeeping somewhere among the wildflowers and thick brush.

It was on a Friday night, and we were filming a party scene when a girl walked in and said there was 'a very big kitty' in the middle of the fish pond. PC was back! And as much hassle as all of us had at the hands (paws) of that damn bobcat, we were all thrilled to see his safe return.

I have to admit, PC could be a handful and get into trouble, but it was mischievous, funny bobcat trouble, and I wouldn't trade my many years with him for anything in the world. He was the beginning of my deep, passionate love for big cats. With PC I learned that people and animals could form a bond as deep and real as could two humans. His emotions were the same as yours and mine. He was capable of very deep love and commitment, and he showed it openly. We formed a tight bond on the drive home from the zoo where we purchased him, and it remained unbroken until his death twenty years later. He also showed boredom, embarrassment, curiosity, indifference—just like we do.

After the movie was completed and the film crew had moved out, it took at least two weeks to restore Sandstone back to normal. Their departure opened up more living space in the main house as well as some of the cottages. Our grocery bill dropped enormously, thank God! As did our use of paper products, toilet paper, napkins, Kleenex, paper towels, and so on. Dear Janice soon had our lawns and foliage back to the lushness we all enjoyed, and PC had visually calmed down—as had John! Neither one of them liked to be surrounded by a lot of strangers. The three of us spent a great deal of time in our motor home, relaxing and recuperating. John and I agreed that the movie was, in a way, the climax of Sandstone. We had pretty much decided by this time to move on. We both felt like our experiment had been a success.

So, after a lot of discussion and soul-searching, we put Sandstone on the market. It sold right away, but after a few weeks we realized the would-be buyers weren't quite as financially solvent as we had been led to believe. The deal fell through. We had several more offers, but somehow they just didn't work out to our satisfaction. One night John and I were talking, and I remember I said to him, "You know, I don't think Sandstone is going to let us go until it finds a new owner who will put it to the same use that we did!" That might sound a little strange to some people, but unless they had actually lived at Sandstone they could never understand how truly magical it was.

"You may be right, pumpkin." He grinned and gave my hand a squeeze. "Yes indeed, you just may be right! What happened here in the four years of operation was so totally unique and involved such very special people I don't think it can ever be duplicated."

I know for me, personally, Sandstone opened up my mind to androgyny. In the beginning, I didn't know where my sexual pathway was headed; I just intuitively knew I was advancing positively toward inner wholeness. This was the sixties, and psychedelic drugs were all the rage (thanks to Timothy Leary and the Beatles), so of course I indulged in frequent LSD trips with John and a few intimate friends and lovers. It was extremely important to drop acid in a safe, trustworthy, calm, and loving environment, so what better place than Sandstone? Just the natural beauty of the surrounding canyons; lush vegetation; abundance of wildflowers; and sparkling, musical water of the fountain wrapped itself around me and embraced me in a warm blanket of security. So did the group of close, loving friends who were there with a warm hand clasp, a soothing touch, and availability should I need them. The incredible sensation opened up my consciousness and unlocked some of my repressed sexuality. The positive environment of Sandstone provided tremendous support for me to continue unlocking and examining my own sexuality. It felt like a black cloud had been lifted from my psyche, and I was more energized by life than ever before. Discovering (and admitting) I was bisexual helped me to become more and more turned on to life itself. And a surprising bonus was the fact that more people were then turned on to me! Remember, I had always been sexually attracted to women, but I was also deeply attracted to and satisfied by men. The term *bisexual* was new to me, as was androgyny. For the first few months of admitting I was bisexual, I still had a very difficult time finding women to have sex with me. But after a few LSD trips, my new openness attracted more women.

And even though this was physically satisfying and I always appeared sexy, I didn't always feel sexy. I continued to be nurtured sexually by both male and female partners, thinking perhaps I could grow my sexuality by having sex with a large number of well-selected people. It didn't work, of course, because I was looking outside of myself for answers when my real focus needed to be within. You know the old adage—"If it is to be, it is up to me!"

It was not until the late seventies, when June Singer wrote two books about this subject, that I began to truly understand and get answers to questions I had always been curious about. *Androgyny* is a book full of psychological and spiritual insights that speak to today's sexual confusion. A person can at once embrace complementary and contradictory attitudes toward sex and gender. Consciousness of our own androgyny can lead to a new sense of personal unity within the larger universe. It's no accident that men and women today are expressing previously undeveloped sides of their natures and taking on roles generally assigned to the opposite sex. Women are thriving in the business world, becoming CEOs of large corporations, and owning their own businesses, while men are equally fulfilled and excelling as stay-at-home dads, content to nurture and keep the home fires burning.

The fact that I'm bisexual doesn't mean that I'm weird or kinky or cursed in any way. It simply means I am fulfilling who I am as a whole human being. My goal for the past several decades has been to live my life as androgynously as possible! By this I mean to have the female and male parts within me connect to my psyche without conflict of any kind. That process has been growing inside me for most of my life, and as a result I am sure of myself, of my leadership, and of my sexuality. I have learned to take responsibility for myself, and this has given me a life of love and happiness. There's no longer any room in my world for anger, hate, greed, pettiness, jealousy, or selfishness.

I've done a great deal of reading and research, and it's pretty clear that we, as a species, are in trouble. The hard facts and trends presented by philosophy, religion, sociology, psychology, ethnology, and other bodies of knowledge that address the human condition all agree that we're in trouble. Research shows that the average person feels a deep level of frustration and despair. It seems we're all immersed in a chaotic, self-made environment characterized by senseless warfare, dehumanizing economics, uncaring authoritarian politics, and cultural institutions that demonstrate the most insane kind of hypocritical dichotomy.

People seem to have a deep capacity for self-deception even though those imagined dreams are sometimes disturbed by brief glimpses of reality. And it's that reality that scares the hell out of everyone! They want change, and yet they're afraid to make changes within themselves. All my life I wanted love. That's all. I just wanted people to love me—but it wasn't until I learned to love myself that anyone else wanted to love me. Sounds pretty simple, doesn't it? Well, just try it! It's a hell of lot harder than you think! If you go around saying, "Wow, I really love myself! I'm terrific and worthy of your love," then you're afraid people will think you're conceited and full of yourself and nobody will want to be around you. It all comes down to balance. You have to bring into balance the male and female parts of yourself in order to make a full, functioning human being. It took me a long time to understand that communication is the key. Without communication there can be no bonding. At Sandstone we discovered the best way to communicate between consenting adults was open sexuality. This involved, but didn't require, nudity. If everyone is nude, there are no status symbols, no sense that another person's clothes are better or more expensive than yours. If someone is in uniform, it labels them as a police officer or soldier or a member of some other group, and therefore people react to them differently. So we're back to open communication, which leads to open sexuality. If a man or woman cannot openly allow his or her mate to enjoy sex with another partner, that smacks of a feeling of ownership and possession. One human being cannot own another. Didn't good old Abe Lincoln settle that question more than a century ago?

It seems that I too had settled a long-asked question. According to Bob Rimmer, "Barbara Williamson has personally validated the

Sandstone philosophy that women can be sexy and sexually active throughout their lifetime." It's true. I'm in my seventies and still enjoy sex as much as I ever did!

I got to thinking about that. Why can't people just let go? Throw the old rules out the window and engage in a little playful pleasure without a thought about procreation? That's so Old Testament! Can you imagine what shape the world would be in if everyone just had sex to create babies? My God! We would be ass-deep in children! The world is already so overpopulated it's scary. People need to be aware now before we breed ourselves into extinction. Besides, fucking is fun! It feels great. It releases tension and enhances all our pleasure points.

A recent article claimed that humans are as hypersexual as Bonobo Apes, but they don't act on it. They repress it and live by the sexual mores that are forced upon them—no matter how frustrating and constricting they are. It's like that wonderful line from the movie *Auntie Mame* when the marvelously flamboyant, sexually free Mame proclaims, "Life is a banquet, and most poor fools are starving to death!"

Early on I became dedicated to opening my heart and mind to overcome the dreadful and widespread disease that I knew was diminishing my human potential—the anti-sex position. I knew I was a sexual being, but because of all I knew about sex, I felt ashamed. I thought it was wrong, and it made me feel awkward when engaging in intercourse. Luckily, I very soon discovered I just wasn't having as much sex as I should be having! Without owning my sexuality, my individual self was at risk.

Thanks to all the powers that be, I hit the sexual jackpot when I met and married my life partner, John, the messiah of sex! It was like stepping into the sunshine after a long, dark winter. Together we created Sandstone so we would have an appropriate environment to express ourselves as freely as a pair of carefree wood nymphs. The incredible beauty of Topanga Canyon pampered our souls, and the soft, warm breeze caressed our naked bodies. More than once as I lay sated in a lover's arms, I thought dreamily, *This must be what the Garden of Eden felt like ...*

With john, I finally understood that my body should be cherished, that I should be loved and adored. I don't like to admit it, but I had a hell of time accepting that humankind was basically good. I hadn't seen much evidence of it thus far in my life, and I had to retrain myself to trust. That's what Sandstone did for me; it stimulated my entire sensory system, and I discovered that I needed touching to feed my soul just as I needed food to feed my body. Sandstone was a safe, intimate, open, and trusting environment where everyone could relax, shed our clothes, romp naked in the sunshine, and feel good about ourselves. We were all free to explore our bodies with each other and feel completely guilt-free in doing so. Watching others engage in sex and sharing your own primary partner with someone else magically overcame any feelings of jealousy.

My sexuality is at the very core of my spiritual and physical being, and it requires a lot of loving and nurturing to maintain. That's what Sandstone did for me and for most of the members and guests who passed through its doors. Through the years, I have been thanked countless times for making the Sandstone experience available to others, and everyone always says the same thing: "We will never forget Sandstone—never!"

Chapter 11

FINALLY, IN DECEMBER OF 1972, we received an offer on the property that met our asking price. It was from a group that would operate as an alcohol recovery retreat, and both John and I felt comfortable with their goals. We both sighed an enormous sigh of relief and promptly began to plan a going-away party. On December 19, 1972, we sent a letter to all Sandstone members advising them that Sandstone would permanently close its doors effective December 28 and inviting them for one last farewell party. In part, the letter stated, "In so many ways, we regret this, as the club has been a great source of fulfillment, learning, and pleasure. It has been everything, in fact, except financially viable. In all our years of operation, a rapidly increasing deficit (mostly from lengthy court battles with the county in order to stay open) has been compensated from personal capital. It is no longer possible to operate in this way. It is our intention to refund any unused portions of membership fees where applicable as soon as the sale is concluded. We will advise you of future plans, including the possibility of reestablishing Sandstone under somewhat different conditions. So let's say good-bye the Sandstone way—come on up to the ranch and let's party hardy!"

And come they did. Upon first arriving, their mood was always quiet and somber, almost as if they were attending a funeral, but as the clothes came off and cocktails flowed, people began grouping together and exchanging stories of their experiences at sandstone. Laughter rang far into the night, and warm hugs were the order of the day. Only two members requested their refunds. Phone numbers and addresses were exchanged and promises made to keep in touch.

Ironically (and simultaneously) the federal government and the Nixon administration claimed the Santa Monica Mountains as a National Park—which immediately killed our property sale due to rezoning. This left us without any support from our members and no cash to sustain ownership of Sandstone. It was headed straight into foreclosure.

I admit my heart plummeted at this realization. It didn't feel like a dignified end to the essence of Sandstone. It felt tawdry and tacky somehow—as if a beloved child was being held in the criminal justice system through no fault of its own.

However, the alcohol recovery group wasn't about to give up; they really loved and wanted Sandstone. They were able to pay us a few thousand dollars on the purchase price and began to move recovering alcoholics into the ranch in 1973. One of Sandstone's members, therapist and US Marine Paul Paige, rounded up a couple of investors, and together they paid us enough to settle the foreclosure with the bank. Effective January 1, 1974, Sandstone was under new ownership. The property was refurbished and officially reopened on April 1, 1974. Marty Zitter and Sue were hired to operate this new venture. The opening brought in some pretty high-profile people and was billed as "A Day of Gay and a Night of Comfort," meaning a day with Gay Talese and a night with Alex Comfort. It was a huge success, and Paul Paige made a conditional promise to Marty that Sandstone would ultimately be formed as a nonprofit organization and function as a therapeutic center. Sadly, Paul reneged and Marty resigned. Paul soon realized that the property could not support itself, and he and his associates were forced to sell. I tried to follow the fate of Sandstone for several years. Somehow, I just couldn't let it go. There were too many joyful memories, too much love, and I had learned so much about myself while living there. I felt I had come into my own at Sandstone. I knew who I was and how I wanted to live my life. I was at peace with the choices I had made. My heart was wide open to receive love, and I finally felt worthy to accept it no matter what form it came in. My bobcat PC taught me that a deep bond of love could exist between animal and human, and John taught me that love between a man and woman could be richer when shared with other loving partners. There's no such thing as too much love.

Now John and I faced an uncertain future. On one hand, it felt incredible to be free of the hassles of maintaining Sandstone—the constant need for money to keep our doors open, the bullshit heaped upon us from the bureaucrats who seemed always to be nipping at our heels, and the enormous responsibility of keeping our hundreds of members and guests happy. We were both filled with a new sense of lightness, an excited anticipation of where the road would lead. We packed everything of importance in our motor home, which consisted mostly of clothes, toiletries, a few kitchen items for cooking, and of course our beloved PC. We left behind all the furniture, paintings, bed linens, and so on and just walked away, locking the door behind us. As I slid into the seat next to John and we started moving down the driveway, I was suddenly filled with a numbness that spread from head to toe. I wanted to turn my head for one last look at the ranch house, the fountain, and the beautiful vegetation, but I didn't. I couldn't. I just stared straight ahead as John maneuvered the big motor home down the narrow, winding road that we had traveled so many times in the past four years, the road that John had graded dozens of times to keep it smooth and available for our guests. Years later, I realized I had blocked out a lot about our last days at Sandstone. The memories and loss were just too painful.

John and I had traveled through Montana several times, and we both loved the wildness of the land, the towering majesty of the trees, the snow-capped mountains in the distance, the density of vegetation that banked both sides of the highway. The air was so crisp and clean it filled our lungs with new life. Even though we had lived high in the Santa Monica Mountains, once we entered the lowlands, thick smog lay like an ugly brownish-yellow blanket all the way to Los Angeles. Driving through the highlands of Montana was a delightful treat. I remember taking deep breaths, filling my lungs and slowly exhaling, ridding myself of the toxic particles of the Los Angeles smog.

We were able to take an option on a couple hundred acres of land situated on the Flathead River. We were told it was the last wild river in the state of Montana. This area was occupied by the Flathead Indians until the white man came and drove them onto reservations in the 1800s. Our property was located right across from the famous Glacier National Park, so we would be reasonably close to civilization should an emergency arise. John parked the motor home among a copse of towering pines and redwoods, and the moment I stepped out and filled my lungs with sweet, clean air, I felt reborn. My feet sank into the soft, spongelike bed of pine needles and moss, and I swear it was every bit as luxurious and plush as our thick, soft carpet in Sandstone. I longed to rip off my clothes, kick off my shoes, and run naked and barefoot through the forest. Ever since leaving Sandstone, I had been fidgeting and scratching, tugging at my jeans and shirt. It felt totally unfamiliar and very confining to wear clothes after living freely nude for so many years. But it was March, with a definite chill in the air, so I kept my knickers on!

One of our former members and Sandstone chef, Doug, had gone to Montana as well, so he pitched a tent behind our motor home. We hadn't been there very long before we had a visit from a ranger from Glacier National Park. He wanted to advise us on rules of safety. Bears were plentiful in the area and would stop at nothing to get their paws on food—any kind of food, but especially bacon.

"Those little rascals can smell bacon cooking a mile away," he said, "so just be careful. Don't make the mistake of thinking how cute they are. Simply because they look like cuddly teddy bears does not mean you can pet them. They're wild animals, and they're lethal. If you get into a scrap with a bear, the bear is the one who will walk away."

"We've had two mama bears with cubs hanging around for the last few days," I said. "We've caught them going through our trash, but they run away when they see us."

"As they become accustomed to your presence, they won't run away," the ranger said. "And you'll wish to hell they did! So just be smart, folks, and use your common sense. Bury your trash, keep your food in an airtight container, and don't do anything stupid!" He grinned and touched the brim of his hat, and I couldn't help but think what a cutie he was in his smart ranger uniform! If this had been Sandstone, I would have invited him to stay awhile!

A few days later, about five o'clock in the morning, I was awakened by PC streaking across my body and diving under the bed. I could hear a series of little growls coming from him and quickly sat up and looked around to find the source of his discomfort. And there it was, filling the window of the motor home. About a thousand-pound moose was staring through the window while John and I slept! We locked gazes, and I didn't move a muscle for what seemed like an hour but was probably only a few seconds before he turned and disappeared into the forest.

We made a couple of trips back to Sandstone to transport our bulldozer and dump truck to our new home. They were badly needed to clear the building site we had chosen about a half-mile from where our motor home was parked. It took a lot of backbreaking work that was not without a few mishaps. Doug was cutting down a tree when the chainsaw blade hit a hard, gnarled knot, and it bounced back and cut a pretty big gash in his side that required quite a few stitches but did no lasting damage. John had a run-in with a small pine that was still young and supple enough to bend but not break. It snapped back from its base, smacking John right in the teeth! Thank God no teeth were lost, but he sported a swollen, bruised mouth for the better part of a month.

At last we had a clearing and were able to stand back and look down at the most spectacular view we'd ever seen. At the bottom of this wilderness valley, a churning, swiftly moving river swept through the foliage like an angry serpent. The forest ranger had told us that it was the last truly wild river in the state of Montana. This was where the wild salmon came to spawn and die. Bears, cougars, bobcats, eagles, and other wild critters with a taste for fish lined the banks every season to gorge on the dying salmon before winter set in.

e had spent the summer enjoying this magnificent gift, this wonderful blessing of freedom and joyful fulfillment. At the end of a lazy day, most of it spent fishing in the swift little stream that ran near our front door, we would dine on freshly caught rainbow trout. I would pull out our big, round black skillet and prop it above the campfire John and Doug had built, and within minutes the sizzling sound of trout rolled in cornmeal would fill the forest air. What an amazing taste experience! From water to skillet to mouth—never had anything tasted so good!

It was now fall, and the colors of autumn painted our area with vivid splashes of yellow, lime green, russet, bright red—a riot of incredible beauty. As leaves fell to the ground, they carpeted our front yard like a patchwork quilt. John and I would have happily burrowed in and stayed snug in our motor home through the winter, but we were smart enough to realize that was a foolhardy dream. Winters were brutal and life-threatening in those Montana hills, so reluctantly we went in search of winter quarters. We rented a little chalet on Big Mountain Ski Resort and spent a couple of weeks cutting four cords of firewood to see us through the cold winter months. It was at the bottom of a ski lift, so John and I could sit in our chalet and watch the skiers whiz by in a spray of fresh powder.

Before winter hit us full force, we decided we should invite some friends, filmmakers Jonathan and Bunny, to come for a visit. We wanted to share the breathtaking beauty of our new home with old friends, and I wanted to hear any news of Sandstone. I still hadn't completely let go.

It was like moving thousands of miles away from a dear friend but still wanting to keep in touch.

John had worked his magic with his trusty old bulldozer and cut out a road on the side of the mountain that twisted more than a hundred feet into the sky. Looking down, one could see the rushing river alive with whitecaps that sparkled like diamonds in the sun. The fog that rose along the river bank was surreal, giving it a mystical softness. After meeting Jonathan and Bunny near the bottom, Doug and I walked the mile up to our motor home while John gave Bunny and Jon a ride in the bulldozer bucket. According to both of them, that night was the best, most restful sleep they'd ever had.

The next day dawned bright and crisp with a warm sun that allowed us to walk about in our short sleeves, so we took advantage of it. Bunny and I packed a lunch, a couple of bottles of wine, and a small jar that I had filled with magic mushrooms. When we arrived at the picnic spot, John built a large, roaring campfire, and we gathered around it, sitting cross-legged on the soft forest floor like the Flathead Indians must have sat a century ago.

As the magic mushrooms kicked in, expanding our senses and sending us twirling into an amazing high, our laughter filled the air. Several times, curious squirrels and chipmunks crept to the edge of the clearing to check us out. Jonathan and Bunny filled us in on what had happened to the Sandstone movie. They had remained at Sandstone until the editing was complete; then the film had been released and had gone into distribution, where it was well received. It would take several more years before it was released to all the major theaters. (This is what I later learned about the fate of the Sandstone movie: It played in the chain of UA Theaters scattered across the US, and it was reported that at many theaters, lines formed around the block. It was the first documentary to gross a million bucks. When it played in Memphis, it was reported that Elvis Presley rented the movie theater and had a private showing for himself and a group of friends. He loved it!)

We spent that winter of '74–'75 in our snug little chalet and had a constant stream of visitors to keep us company. Old friends and members of Sandstone continued to visit, and our lifestyle of sex, drugs, and rock 'n' roll kept us warm and happy. We had a huge fireplace that danced with tall, wavering flames all winter long. I can't remember it ever going cold. John kept it fed like a favorite pet, and it kept us warm and cozy through the coldest days.

It was during that time we decided to quit smoking—the nicotine cigarette type of smoking. We continued smoking pot, which helped ease us off the nicotine, and in about three weeks, we had both kicked the habit.

The clean air and simple lifestyle suited us both. We felt rejuvenated and eager to get on with our lives. Unfortunately, we were running out of money. We had no income, and the money we had received from the sale of Sandstone was dwindling rather quickly. I put some feelers out, and an old friend (a VP with IBM) wanted to fund our proposed Project Synergy, a ten-million-dollar project. As talks began, John and I were thrilled. We could have delivered some incredible creative talent that would have put us back into a financially stable position, but the deal fell through. IBM suffered a huge loss that quarter, and he was uncomfortable making an investment at that time. Damn!

Our cherished alternative lifestyle seemed to be coming to an end. We would not be paid for creating a new, healthy, productive, happy way of living. Instead, we seemed to be destined to plod along in the same old stagnant culture that we both despised.

Forced to take inventory, we realized we really had nothing of value. Because of the nudity we both cherished, we didn't even have any clothes—and certainly no cold-weather clothes. The few shirts and jeans and sneakers I owned were made for the warmth of Southern California. In Montana I needed fleece-lined trousers, snow boots, hats, and gloves—very expensive. John's wardrobe was as skimpy as mine. The only member of our family who was properly dressed for the weather was PC with his thick fur coat!

We weren't ready to go back to California, so we headed south to Mobile, Alabama. *What a come down,* I remember thinking. How the mighty had fallen—from our Sandstone mansion to a Mobile, Alabama trailer park! One of the reasons, besides the weather, that John had chosen Mobile was that he had a brother living there and thought perhaps he might be able to lend a helping hand. Wrong! We lived in Mobile for four years and only saw him once. There was no love lost between the brothers. The harsh truth hit us like a sledge hammer: we were facing homelessness.

There was only one thing to do—get a job. This was easy because of my skills in the insurance field, and I was soon (and once again) sitting behind a desk dressed in a business suit and pantyhose. Ugh! Pantyhose! How I hated them. I was forced to buy a few outfits at Goodwill and other thrift stores, and I had to grit my teeth each morning when I put them on. It was unnatural, and I hated every minute I spent dressed in the working woman's uniform! I was seething inside, because I had no choice, no freedom, and the low wages were an insult to my intelligence. My first job paid only $425 per month, barely enough to exist, but I stayed until I could find another, slightly higher- paying position.

John tried his hand at a few different odd jobs, but there wasn't a big demand for a messiah of sex in Mobile, Alabama! We pretty much lived on bologna sandwiches and coffee, but when we did have a couple of extra bucks, we would go to the local Holiday Inn for a decent meal. At those times I couldn't help but think back to the lavishly sumptuous meals we used to serve at Sandstone—beef stroganoff, roasted chicken, shrimp Scampi, New York or porterhouse steaks an inch thick, vegetables and salads so fresh it was almost orgasmic when you bit into them. We befriended a waitress who worked the happy hour shift, and she would heap our plates with tasty hors d'oeuvres, occasionally slipping in a club sandwich or some other goody she could slip by the watchful eye of the manger. But even John's considerable charm only went so far; he had to get a paying gig.

John had gone to the unemployment office several times and had become friends with the woman in charge. Even though she could do nothing for him, she allowed him to occupy a desk and help with job placements. It didn't pay anything, but it gave him something to do with his time and a possible chance of finding something steady. She introduced him to a Special Forces Vietnam veteran, Bill Rowzee, now general manager of Wilson Electric. Owner Joe Wilson was also a major stockholder in the greyhound race track where Bill worked and was quite a wealthy businessman in Mobile. Bill approached Joe about bringing John on board to invent a line of electronic products (one of John's strong suits), and Joe agreed. The first product John proposed was a voice stress analyzer, and Joe agreed to fund it, so John was once again gainfully employed.

Just when I thought it was safe to exhale and not worry so much about finances, our motor home was repossessed. We still owed about $2,500, and I wasn't aware it was up for repossession until the repo guys showed up to claim it. John and I were both at work when they towed it away, which meant that PC was waiting inside for us. I can just imagine the surprise of the Repo guys when they looked inside and found a full-grown bobcat sitting there! The minute we discovered what had happened, we rushed down to the impound lot and rescued our boy. With Bill's help, we found another one-bedroom mobile home, and the three of us moved in and tried to settle down as much as possible under the circumstances. At least we were now a two-income household and things were finally looking up financially.

I really don't remember much of those years we spent in Mobile, because the culture was so foreign to me. I disliked it so much. I just put my head down and plowed on, determined to get out of this horrible slump we were in. I never doubted for a moment that we would survive and succeed. That's what we did best!

Chapter 12

IN RETROSPECT, I GUESS ONE of the reasons it was so grim during those years spent in Mobile was the memories of Sandstone that flooded my mind, refusing to fade. I remember one particular gray, rainy day when I was standing in the closet-sized kitchen, spreading some saltine crackers with a thin layer of catsup. This would be our appetizer until I made dinner in a few minutes—after I rid myself of blouse, bra, panties, skirt and the dreaded pantyhose that dug into my waist and itched like crazy. Maybe a little self-pity took over, because I suddenly had a biblical vision of John and I, blissfully naked, relaxed on a soft bed of grass in the Garden of Eden, and then suddenly and violently cast into hell. I know that sounds pretty dramatic, but those are the kinds of thoughts and images that filled my head. One montage that I remember clearly was of a herd of beautiful mustangs running wild and free in a meadow of wildflowers, manes flowing, nostrils flaring, stallions and mares alike, sharing a bond of freedom.

After changing into a caftan and a pair of old slippers, I went to the tiny refrigerator and took out a plastic baggie of raw chicken necks for PC. John and I would dine on bologna sandwiches and white Wonder Bread. Gone were the days of thinly sliced ham piled high on a bed of spicy mustard, crisp lettuce, juicy tomatoes, and seven-grain wheat bread. The only thing wonderful about white Wonder Bread was its price of twenty-seven cents a loaf! I shuddered to think what it was doing to our arteries!

As I moved to the tiny counter to make the sandwiches, a trio of cockroaches the size of golf balls scurried from the corners and darted across my cutting board. The roaches in Alabama were so huge I told John I was going to find a saddle and ride them! I was sick to death of seeing them and hearing their moist little hisses when cornered. I slammed the knife down on the counter and said, "All right, you little pricks, get the hell out of my kitchen!" They disappeared in less than a second, and I gave a triumphant chortle.

"What are you laughing about?" John asked.

"I think I'm losing it—I was just talking to some bugs!"

"I think we're both a little buggy at this point," he laughed. "But don't worry, pumpkin, this is just a temporary situation."

I knew that was true. Neither one of us had ever placed too much importance on possessions. As long we had each other and PC, we were content. Each time we moved, the new space required different furnishings, but I found we could do quite nicely with a dining table and chairs, a few dishes, a couple of pots and pans, a skillet, and of course a TV. Don't get me wrong—I do love beautiful things, and it is ever so much nicer to live in luxury rather than poverty, but just knowing that I didn't need it gave me a sense of self. The things I did need in my life were spiritual enlightenment, love, compassion, joy, meditation, and mindfulness. Our culture has been brainwashed into believing that having a lot of money is the answer to everything. Make as much money as quickly as possible—that's the American dream. I think that's why our culture is morally bankrupt.

In late 1977, Wilson Electric no longer wanted to fund the electronic project John and Bill were involved with. Apparently the field of electronics was beyond understanding for most Southerners. It was way too risky! So John and Bill set up their own company called Psycho-Science and went into business for themselves. (We joked that Bill was the psycho and John was the science!) By this time I had doubled my salary handling insurance claims, and we finally had enough money to lease a little house. We were no longer eating bologna for dinner, but I was still far from content. What had happened to that beautiful alternate lifestyle that we had so carefully honed at Sandstone? It had been our haven for personal growth and development and limitless potential.

Almost every radio station in Mobile played country-western music, and every time Freddy Fender's hit song "Wasted Days and Wasted Nights" came on, we cracked up and promptly dubbed it our song.

I'm sure the denizens of Mobile thought we were from another planet, with our new wave views and our laid-back West Coast demeanor. We had accumulated a handful of friends, transplants all, who no doubt appeared as strange as we did. Paula and Jack were from New York City, taking a sabbatical in Mobile. Paula was originally from Mobile, as was John, so they had something in common from the start. Jack did sculpture work and was recruited to do videos for Psycho-Science. All of us were in our late thirties and had the same artistic mind-set. (Some time later, Paula would appear in the Guinness World Book of Records for creating the world's largest photographs. Life magazine commissioned her to photograph the final Ringling Bros. Barnum & Bailey tiger show with esteemed trainer Gunther Williams. I have one of those photographs hanging on my living room wall today; it's my pride and joy.)

Paula and Jack had become so overwhelmed by the fast pace of New York City they both badly needed a respite. But after spending a year in Mobile, Paula called to say, "I must get out of here." Paula told me, "I find myself waking up every morning and feeling for my breasts to make sure I am still a woman!" I related instantly. I was trying so hard not to let myself sink into a state of depression. The culture shock had left me reeling, but if that wasn't enough, the nearly tropical weather finished me off. There was so much humidity in the air I sweated from morning till night. I constantly felt sticky, and my energy level was at the lowest point it had ever been. I simply dragged myself about, and it even affected my voice; I found myself slipping into the slow drawl of a Southerner, dropping the *g*'s at the ends of words because it took less energy! While writing this book, I had to really search for something positive to say about Mobile, and the only thing I could come up with was this: I didn't have to wear pantyhose! Shorts and a tee were fine for out of doors, and most women wore a light cotton blouse and trousers for their air-conditioned offices.

Paula and Jack rented a huge, beautiful antebellum house on Government St. in one of the nicer areas of Mobile. John and I loved spending time with them, and it gave us a chance to get out of our small dwelling and stretch our legs, so to speak. The house had a wrap-around balcony in front, and we loved to sit out with our feet propped upon the wrought-iron railing and watch the Mardi Gras parade go by. Held annually on Shrove Tuesday, the last day before lent, it is celebrated by carnivals, masquerade balls, and long parades of costumed merrymakers. Of course, it was just a local Mardi Gras; the world-famous Mardi Gras held in New Orleans was a week-long affair that attracted party-goers from all over the globe.

It seems I had a knack for attracting psychos no matter which coast I lived on, and I guess the name of John and Bill's venture, Psycho-Science, was some sort of magnet. Anyway, one day a beautiful young woman named Brenda showed up at the door and offered her services as a volunteer gardener. She was an artist and writer, quite engaging and obviously possessing a rather high IQ. She loved working in the soil, she claimed, and it was soon apparent she did indeed have a green thumb. The flower bed in front of the building became lush with a variety of flowers and shrubs artistically arranged.

Brenda was married to a very handsome young man who didn't seem to have much going for him except his good looks. He was naïve and just a tad shallow but likeable. It wasn't long before I recognized the signs: she was sexually attracted to John and brazen enough to go to his office and try to seduce him. John was amused (and intrigued), so he invited her to have a threesome with us, which she readily accepted. She was really a gorgeous woman with an overwhelming zest for life and a delightful personality—as well as a killer body! We bonded right away, as she wanted to leave the South as badly as we did. "I just want to get the hell out of here," she would sigh. "I want to go someplace exciting—I want to be *somebody!*"

I felt a little spark of hope flicker inside me. Maybe, just maybe, she was the woman I'd been looking for to complete and fill the void in our relationship. Remember, that had always been my goal. I knew that a well- functioning threesome, a triangle, was the strongest and most synergistic bond between lovers. I had been searching for just such a relationship ever since I had discovered my attraction for women. I loved John dearly, but I also craved the softness of a female companion in my life. The dynamics between the three of us were so strong and exciting and the sex was great, so I let myself believe (or hope) Brenda wanted the same things. The fact that she'd never had the Sandstone experience made it a little difficult to explain, but Brenda seemed open to learning.

During this time John began receiving quite a lot of publicity, which attracted Jack Welch from Akron, Ohio. He and his attorney scheduled a meeting with John and Bill to look over their patents and products. He told them how impressed he was and made an incredible offer that would ultimately pay us ten million bucks! We were blown away by the offer and so eager and desperate to get out of Alabama (one of the conditions of the deal was that we move to Akron, Ohio) that we jumped on board without a second thought—and without a minute of research! You know the old adage—if it sounds too good to be true …

Needless to say, we fell for Jack's bullshit and loaded up our motor home and moved to Akron—and Brenda went with us. She simply said bye-bye to her handsome husband, and we became the threesome I'd always wanted. I won't go into all the intricate details (what a mess!), but we soon discovered there were more crooks in Akron than we'd ever encountered anywhere! It seems the huge, successful company Jack had bragged about was really owned by his cousin and Jack had no say about anything! This was quite a blow to John and me, because we always took people at face value, believing them to be as honest and fair as we were. Bottom line: the only thing John got out of the big deal was a Mercedes Benz SLC and a couple of years' salary. The only thing that helped us settle in Akron was a phone call out of the blue from the William Morris Agency in New York informing us we had a check due from Gay Talese's book *Thy Neighbor's Wife* in the amount of fifty thousand dollars! Gay received a record breaking amount of $2.3 million from United Artists' purchase of the movie rights. The payment to John and I was for the use of our names in any future movie(s) that would be made.

Okay, finally no more bologna sandwiches, but even as our financial situation was stabilizing, our home life was falling apart. It was becoming more obvious each day that our beautiful Brenda had some serious mental problems; she was schizophrenic and psychotic. I was always very patient and gentle with Brenda, confident that if I could help her understand the true meaning of androgyny (understanding and experiencing the female and male parts within), we could live in peace and harmony and integrate ourselves into a oneness. But that old green-eyed monster, jealousy, reared its ugly head. She was in love with John and very jealous of the solid bond between the two of us. When her attempts to break us up failed, she would throw psychotic fits, crying and raging and then storming out to return to Mobile and her long-suffering husband.

She would always call a few weeks later, tearfully begging us to take her back. And we always did. I knew she had been emotionally damaged as a child, and I was willing to help her work through those issues, but it was becoming more and more difficult to deal with her outbursts. She was very talented as a writer, and I thought perhaps if she had a project to concentrate her energy on she would feel useful and needed. We were still having sex, and even though I knew she loved John, she still responded to me enthusiastically and with a great show of affection. I suggested we start working on a book together. I'd always wanted to write about Sandstone, and I thought perhaps Brenda would understand everything more clearly if we were putting it all down on paper. Everything was going smoothly until one Sunday morning when John asked us if we wanted to go out to brunch. Brenda pouted and sulked, whining that she wanted to go out with just John, and why did it always have to be the three of us going out together?

John just smiled and told her we were going out for breakfast and she could join us or not; it was her choice.

She chose to stay home, and when we returned a couple of hours later, we found a large canvas (she kept her art supplies in the basement) with a fire-breathing devil surrounded by angry flames. She was a very talented artist, so the painting felt real—and also very disturbing. And there she sat on the sofa, as smug as a canary-eating pussycat, completely bald. She had shaved her head! That was the proverbial last straw. We asked her to leave. I bought her a wig and a plane ticket back to Mobile, and she tearfully waved good-bye as she boarded the plane. I hated to see her go. She was talented, brilliant, and gorgeous—but a complete nutcase.

Both John and I were bitterly disappointed by the way things had turned out in Akron. Jack Welch was a fraud. Within a couple of years he had driven the company into bankruptcy. Every promise he had made to John and Bill fell through. Nothing was as it should have been. I know John and Bill felt like fools for falling for this guy's line of bullshit, but they were honest men and just naturally expected honesty in return. Jack was hooked on Demerol and had always done a few lines of cocaine every so often, but it soon became a habit, and his life quickly spiraled out of control. I'm not going to go into all the details; they are far too numerous and frustrating. Let's just say John and I couldn't wait to pack and get the hell out of Dodge!

We put our house on the market (we had bought a little place a couple of years before not only to live in while we were there but also, hopefully, as an investment) and we were thinking that the sale would bring in enough money to see us through until we decided where we wanted to settle. This was in 1982, and the economy had taken a nosedive. We discovered there was a glut of more than five thousand homes with foreclosure and for-sale signs on their lawns. No way were we going to stick around and wait for the market to recover! We had about $33,000 equity in the place, so we were able to surrender the house keys to the bank and walk away battered and bruised but not defeated. In an attempt at levity in such a grim situation, I quoted Horace Greeley's quip: "Go west, young man—go west to find your fortune!"

John pulled me down on his lap and laughed. "California or bust! I heard pumpkins thrive in the California sunshine!"

So we were back on track and apparently headed for another adventure. PC took his place by the side window in the motor home and watched the countryside speed by. John and I agreed that perhaps Southern California was just a tad too hot, so we'd take a look at the northern part of that beautiful state. We took our time driving, stopping every so often if some roadside attraction caught our attention or PC needed to stretch his legs. It was a leisurely trip. We needed time to catch our breath and recover from the financial and personal beating we had experienced in Akron. I'll tell you this: we had both lost a lot of respect for and trust in our fellow man. For a couple of peace-loving free spirits, it was very difficult to admit we were becoming skeptical and suspicious. God! How my heart ached for the serenity of Sandstone!

We took a swing through Washington State and stayed for a few months in North Bend. Money was a little low, so I took a temporary position selling insurance (always my strong suit) while John worked with a venture capitalist to create new products. As his new deal began to fall into place, we moved to San Jose, California. This was late in '83, and by the first of the New Year I was hired by Phoenix Mutual as a supervisor and went into sales, where the big money was.

Much to my surprise and completely out of the blue, Brenda called John and asked if she could come back and try again. She missed us, she said, and was miserable in Mobile, Alabama. She'd always wanted to go to California. I suspected she had stars in her eyes and thought that her incredible beauty would lead to a career in show business. Her past erratic behavior was troubling, and I didn't trust her. I told John an emphatic no, but my gentle, kindhearted mate believed in second chances (and third and fourth!) so he agreed to let her come home—but with a condition. She would have to seek therapy. Her mother had done a real number on her, and she was one fucked- up, sick little girl. I knew she was looking for a place to belong and someone to belong with. I admit I had loved having her as a part of my family. I thought I had found a life mate, someone who would fill that part of me that needed a woman's love. I tried to forget her schizophrenic disorder, foolishly believing that love could cure her and make her whole. John found a Jungian therapist, and the first session seemed to go quite well. However, like a puppy that has been kicked so often it knows only the feel of the boot, Brenda called her mother and told her where she was and that she was now in therapy and living with John and me. She needed answers to her childhood, and this freaked out her mom. No way was she going to allow Brenda to air childhood secrets and abuse! She ordered her to come back to Alabama at once and within a few days had sent Brenda a plane ticket.

And so she left—this bright, beautiful girl with so much potential who was so emotionally damaged it had crippled her for life. To this day, I still think about her with a deep sense of loss.

I threw myself into work, and by the end of 1985 I had secured enough income (more than $100,000) to be widely recognized in the company and awarded the honor of Agent of the Year. In the next two years I acquired a sales group of five women and one man in my unit, and we ranked number one in volume of sales in the thirteen-state western region.

By 1989 I was financially stable enough to buy a lovely home in the Santa Cruz Mountains. I'd always loved to be surrounded by nature, and this was an incredibly beautiful area. Once again I was fortunate to wake up to sounds of song birds outside my window and the scurrying little paws of squirrels and chipmunks searching for pine nuts that had fallen from the trees surrounding my property. A sense of contentment settled over John as well, and soon we were having Sandstone-type parties. What a relief to shed my clothes and feel the air on my body, which had for too long been forced into pantyhose, binding clothes, and closed shoes.

As the nineties rolled around, we settled into a lifestyle more befitting to our needs. At first the parties were a mixture of both men and women, but soon the men no longer seemed necessary. I'm not even sure when or how it happened, but suddenly our weekend parties consisted of a dozen women—and John! This was perfectly acceptable to the messiah of sex! And me? I felt like a kid in a candy store with an unlimited budget! There was so much laughter and affection filling our house in those years. I was very happy and content with all the women who shared my bed. There was a gentleness and a great tenderness about our lovemaking that I will cherish always.

As I've said many times, money was never that important to me. It wasn't a driving force in my life but merely a necessity. My main goal was to make enough money for us to live on for the rest of our lives. I managed to achieve this in just eleven years, and that is quite a feat for anyone! Now we had to decide where we wanted to spend our golden years.

Chapter 13

WE BOTH LOVED THE DESERT and started thinking about Nevada. I was still working in the insurance business, so it was up to John to do the research and scouting for a new home for us. We were so attuned to each other's likes and dislikes I knew that whatever he decided on I would love as well. Our one requirement was that it be an oasis of calmness with a small population but close enough to a town where we would be assured of necessary services should we need them. We wanted a place where there were no fires, floods, or earthquakes—we'd had quite enough of Mother Nature's wrath in the past few years!

In July of '94 we purchased a three-bedroom modular home on ten acres in Fallon, Nevada. It was located at the base of the Stillwater Mountain range, not too far from the Reno Airport but far enough away from the urban sprawl to afford us the peace and quiet we both felt we needed at this juncture of our lives. The ten acres of seemingly endless desert were as flat as the proverbial pancake but still oddly beautiful. It was surrounded on all sides by towering mountains that gave us an incredible panoramic view. I was really anxious to move in, but the place required a lot of work to make it habitable. I stayed in the Bay Area and continued my work while John took care of the construction and refurbishing. In April of '95 he moved into the new house and began adding the buildings and workshops he wanted, and I spent as much time as I could visiting. It seemed a long haul, because we had never been separated during our many years together. Both of us had always appreciated the land and loved to be surrounded by the sights and sounds of nature. Where once I had marveled at all the little critters that lived in the lush, dense forests of trees and shrubs, I now had a whole new set of creatures to admire. Jack rabbits with their unusually long back legs bounded across our backyard like so many kangaroos. Dust-colored prairie dogs gave off high-pitched barks as they dug numerous burrows and bred like rodents. Sleekly feathered roadrunners zipped like rockets, emitting their unusual call and then skidding to a halt long enough to dip their long beaks into the hot sand and pull out a wriggling reptile for lunch. I knew, of course, that there were also rattlesnakes, Gila monsters, and tarantulas living in holes and under rocks, but I successfully put them out of my mind. I was amazed by the number of beautiful desert songbirds. Their clear, melodic trills could be heard for miles across the flat expanse of desert. Red-headed woodpeckers as large as squirrels drummed away at every tree trunk they encountered, no matter how short and stunted the tree. The gnarled pine trees at the base of the mountains, twisted by years of wind, dotted the horizon and housed a whole roster of tiny creatures. Coyotes yip-yipped far into the night, and in the high canyons of the Stillwater Mountains herds of mule deer raised their young.

In August of '95, John's handyman, Richard, told him about a small group of big cats who were being housed at a highway patrolman's property awaiting eviction or euthanasia, whichever came first. John was outraged by what he considered senseless murder and immediately contacted the proper authorities, promising to have a compound for the exotic big cats within the thirty-day period allotted by law. And he did! With the help of several kindhearted animal lovers, he erected a new dwelling for three cougars, one tiger, one lion, and a big old flop-eared dog! Tiger Touch was born.

I'll never forget the first weekend I went to Fallon after the big cats moved in. I was amazed at their acceptance of me. You could almost see the gratitude and appreciation in their eyes. I know they knew they had been saved from death. A sense of peace and completion washed over me and I felt more content than I had in a long time. This was where I belonged. This was what I was destined to do with my life. After dinner, I wandered outside to watch the sun go down and stood gazing at the primitive beauty of the sprawling desert. Big rocks toned red, russet, and brown by the slanting sun rose majestically in the far distance. The sky was still very blue, bleaching to burnished silver at the horizon where the haze of the evening married it to the soil. I was suddenly jolted by a memory so strong it swept through my entire body. That huge painting of the desert in John's office the first day I met him! And the promise he'd made: "Come with me, Barbara Cramer. I promise you a very interesting life …" The promise had been kept.

I must admit I was feeling a little envious that John got to stay in Fallon with the cats while I still toiled away in the Bay area. Of course, he tried to make me as much a part of the newly founded Tiger Touch as possible with so much distance between us. I was chafing at the bit to finally retire and move into my new home on a full-time basis. There had been a lot of local publicity about Tiger Touch, and it had somehow made its way to Indiana. A breeder called me and said they had a young lioness they could no longer care for; did we possibly have room for her at Tiger Touch? Of course we did!

This was in October of '95, and we were to pick her up at the Reno airport. Several of my girlfriends went with us, and John drove, all of us greatly excited to meet our new family member. As soon as we reached the baggage claim area we could hear the soft, almost pleading roar of a lion—and there she was, Nala, in a large carrier and staring directly at me! It was almost like she was saying, "There you are! Get me out of here!"

Three of us women got into the backseat, and John led Nala to the open door. Without any encouragement at all, she leaped into the truck, settled herself across all three laps, and snuggled in for a nap. She must have been exhausted and frightened after her long flight from Indiana, but her innate sense of survival told her she was safe. As we drove from Reno to Fallon, the moonlight fell through the windows, bathing her shiny coat in a golden glow of beauty. It is one of the most priceless memories I have.

John's latest project was also launched that month. He was building an addition twenty feet wide and sixty feet long alongside our existing home to serve as a sort of recreation area for us. There was a large deck, a hot tub, a guest bedroom; it was a place separate from our living quarters where we could entertain guests and just chill out. One of our neighbors was an excellent artist, and she painted a huge, jungle-themed mural on the back wall, and her mother (talented in the art of stained glass) made an exquisite tiger to go over the door leading out to the deck. We christened the building "Catatat."

By this time I was spending most of my time in Fallon but still commuting to Santa Cruz to service the last of my clients and wind up my business. I also had to find a buyer for our house in Santa Cruz and start packing up for the big move.

Having all those wonderful, beautiful, magnificent cats in my backyard made me miss and long for PC. It was great to go out to the compound and talk to and stroke the cats through the fence, but I wanted a cat I could hold in my arms and cuddle and spoil like I had with PC. Having once shared my life with an exotic cat, there was an emptiness that was almost physical. I had long been curious about the possibility of species bonding. Was it possible for a human and an animal to love one another deeply and unconditionally? There were many times when I felt that with PC, but as much as he loved me, he had always been a daddy's boy. I think he looked upon me as a mother figure. I fed him and snuggled him when he was frightened, and I was the keeper of the gate, the one who said if and when he could go outside. I was also the one to discipline him when he was naughty and to teach him manners that he would rather not have adhered to! He was just a rowdy boy, a prankster, and John encouraged and identified with him on that level. I needed a female who recognized the softer side of love. I wondered if it was possible or if it really made a difference—and I was determined to find out. So I did a little research (I loved researching new projects; it kept my active brain busy and occupied). We were having dinner one night, and I said, "You know, honey, we both miss PC so much, we need to get another cat, an inside cat—don't you agree?"

"Yes, I do. I really miss that little scamp. He filled the house with such life, didn't he?" He laughed. "Okay, you find one, and we'll go take a look at him—"

"Not him, her. I want a female this time. PC was such a daddy's boy, and I want a mama's girl. I want to see if the bond between females is as strong as I think it is."

"What if she turns out to be a daddy's girl?" he teased. "Well, I could share—maybe. Just a little …"

And so it was that I found a breeder of exotic cats in Tehachapi, California. Their Siberian lynx was due to give birth to a litter of cubs in mid-April, so I put my claim in then and there for a female. Now all I had to do was wait. I began counting down the days, feeling very much like I imagined a pregnant woman would feel while awaiting the birth of her baby. I was so excited and shared my news with all my friends. A couple of them suggested I get two cats. Both would be happier with a feline companion. This made sense to me, so I asked around, and someone put me in touch with a breeder in Oregon who had an African serval available.

I admit to a little trepidation, because the lynx and the serval are two distinctly different breeds, and I wasn't sure how they would react to one another. The serval looks like a miniature cheetah with its long, spindly legs and has the reputation of being a love cat, while the lynx, a loner cat, is shorter and stockier; but the way I looked at it, they were both felines and probably had the same sort of temperament. I would soon find out.

In December of '95 we drove to Oregon to pick up the serval. I named him Streaker, because he was as fast as a rocket streaking across the sky. He could leap into the air a good twenty feet and streak up and down the stairs in a nanosecond! The first time I met him he hissed and bit me really hard! So much for the love cat! I knew he was just frightened of his new surroundings and the two new strangers in his life, so he did a lot of defensive hissing and slapping to establish his strength. I would have to catch him and wrap him in a towel or blanket until he calmed down. Then I would cuddle him on my lap until he stopped shaking and realized he was safe. Looking back, that probably wasn't the most ideal time to bring someone new into our home. We were in the middle of settling into our new place, and there's always a lot of confusion during a move, so of course Streaker was upset. But once in the new place he settled in quite nicely. The new carpet was very thick and luxurious, and he loved to roll in the deep, plush pile and knead to his heart's content. He started joining me in bed at night and snuggling close to my warmth. Finally! He was living up to his breed's reputation for being love cats.

The house in Santa Cruz sold in March of '96, and by April I had moved with all our belongings to Fallon and a brand-new way of life. I was just fifty-seven years old and officially retired! I was both excited and a little nervous. Everything in the desert was so different from the lush greenness of California—not just the scenery but the weather as well. It would take some getting used to.

At last that wonderful day in May I'd been waiting for arrived; it was time to pick up my brand spanking new lynx cub. Streaker rode in the backseat of our truck and was a very good boy during the long trip. The mama lynx had had three cubs, the cutest, fluffiest little fur balls I'd ever seen! They were in a holding crib, so the breeder took them out and they toddled about on the floor. They were still a little wobbly at just five weeks old, and I could hardly wait to get my hands on them—but before I could, one little girl approached John and started climbing up his leg. He lifted her to his shoulder, and she snuggled under his chin while I gently stroked her soft, silky fur. I was in love instantly. I carefully took her from John and cradled her against my breast so she could feel the steady beating of my heart. I know this probably sounds weird, but she looked like a female. There was something distinctively feminine about her, and I immediately named her Peggy Sue—a good old-fashioned Southern female name. I hated to let go of her, but I knew she would be safer riding in the small carrier we'd brought with us, so I tucked her inside and put the carrier on the seat next to Streaker. He took one sniff of this new scent and immediately began investigating, pawing lightly at the cage as if inviting her out to play. Peggy Sue showed him what she was made of; she growled and hissed and faced him fearlessly! This tiny baby, one-eighth the size of a strange African serval, held her ground! Several times during the five-hour drive back to Fallon I could hear her growling when Streaker became too much of a pest.

As soon as we got home, I took Peggy Sue out of her carrier and inspected every tiny inch of her, kind of like a new mom checks out her new baby, counting fingers and toes. She was perfect. Her paws were very large, the pads still pinkish and as soft as velvet. Her eyes still held a trace of blue (most babies, including humans, are born with blue eyes) but would soon change into a gorgeous deep gold. I kept her in her carrier for the first three weeks so Streaker wouldn't accidently hurt her. He was a big, rowdy, playful boy, and she was still so tiny that I worried. I took her out to feed her six times a day and also to hold and cuddle her. I wanted to start the bonding procedure as soon as possible. It was also important that Streaker got to know and accept her. The carrier had small openings on all four sides, and the two of them spent a lot of nose-to-nose time together, getting acquainted and becoming familiar with each other's scent. Streaker was dying to get Peggy Sue out of that awful cage so he could run and chase her and teach her some fun cat games, but I was still a little nervous about that. He looked thin and delicate, but when he smacked you with one of his long, pole-like legs, it felt like being whacked by a golf club!

I started letting Peggy Sue out of her carrier for longer periods of time so she could interact with Streaker, still keeping a close eye on them. As it turned out, it wasn't Streaker who hurt Peggy Sue—it was the other way around. If Streaker got too rough, Peggy Sue would sink her growing fangs into his head! This happened three times and required three trips to the vet. Streaker got the message, and from that point on they played together peacefully.

Peggy Sue was the more sociable of the two and loved to hang out when friends came over. There would be maybe a dozen of us lying on the floor, throwing a toy for her, and she would happily chase it as long as we threw it. She had a few favorite people (the ones who brought her catnip for Christmas!), and she would run to greet them when they came over. Streaker lived up to his name; when he heard someone knocking at the door, he would streak into the bedroom and hide under the bed until they left. Eventually Peggy Sue decided she didn't like all that much attention either, and she would join Streaker under the bed until our guests left. She still had a few favorites that she was used to and enjoyed, but she seemed to decide that her immediate family was enough for her.

She loved to ride in the truck with us and would sit regally on the center console, gazing through the windshield. You can imagine how many people stopped and stared and pointed!

One winter we took a short trip to Montana to let them play in the snow. We loaded everything into our motor home and took off, curious to see how they would react to the cold weather and all that white stuff on the ground. Peggy Sue loved it and jumped right into the nearest drift, rolling around and playing. Streaker hated it! His breed preferred warmer weather that was kinder to his short, thin coat, while Peggy Sue's thick, lush coat was made for very cold weather. That's where they came to a parting of the ways, travel wise. Whenever Streaker saw us loading up the motor home, he'd head for his sanctuary under the bed, stubbornly refusing to go anywhere in the RV. He was the eldest and male, so he wanted to call the shots. When we got into bed at night,

Streaker would settle down between us, ready for his snuggling. Peggy Sue wanted to share the love too and would leap on the bed to join us, and he would promptly chase her away. This was extremely infuriating to me, because I was still in the training process with Peggy Sue and wanted her to share my bed and learn to love and accept me as an equal. We finally worked it out, and to this day Peggy Sue and I still share the same bed.

One time when John was out of town on business, Peggy Sue and Streaker took advantage of his absence. The alpha male was gone, so they started romping and chasing each other, jumping on and over furniture, misbehaving like a couple of mischievous kids. The next morning I noticed that Peggy Sue was just sitting staring at me. I finally coaxed her to come to me, and I saw she was limping badly, sort of dragging her right rear leg. There was a swollen lump at the joint, so I loaded her into the truck and whisked her off to the vet. Sure enough, her leg was broken. *My God*, I thought, *what were those two up to while I slept?* The vet set her leg, put it in a cast, and gave me some pain pills, and we were on our way. As soon as we got home I gave her one of the pills, thinking it would probably make her drowsy and she would take a long nap. Wrong! It had the direct opposite effect and wired her instead. She began running through the house, dragging the heavy cast, which thump-thumped on the floor but did not slow her down. When the medication finally wore off, she curled up on the bed and slept for several hours. I had learned my lesson: don't give pain pills to an exotic cat.

The next traumatic incident involved Streaker. John and I were getting their dinner ready, and John stepped outside for a second, leaving the door ajar. Like a streak, our naughty serval zipped through the door, ran around the house a couple of times, charged across the road, and headed for the open desert beyond. My heart almost stopped beating, I was so terrified. The desert was crawling with rattlesnakes and coyotes and any number of dangers that could harm or kill my boy.

Pulling on boots and jackets, John and I started walking into the desert, calling his name, combing every inch of sand and shrubs and prairie-dog holes, searching until dark. Up at dawn the next morning, we searched until we were exhausted. Then it started raining—a real downpour, which was rare at that time of year. Forced to go home, I called everyone I could think of and told them to keep an eye out for Streaker. I can't remember when I've ever been so frightened. I was sure we'd lost him forever. The rain had surely washed away any scent that he would recognize. Then, miracle of all miracles, on the fourth day a neighbor called and said, "Hi, Barbara. I have your cat locked in my trailer. Come and get him."

Apparently he had seen a bunch of chickens in the neighbor's yard. He was hungry and there was dinner, so he went for it! Thankfully, my neighbor had the presence of mind to coax him into her trailer and lock the door. Most women would have thrown their hands in the air and screamed, so I'm very grateful that she called me instead!

When we got the runaway home, Peggy Sue seemed a little pissed off. She sniffed him all over, and it was plain from her expression that she did not like what she smelled. God knows what he'd gotten into, but she didn't like it and kept her distance. He was famished and ate eight chicken legs before pausing to clean his fur. After he had groomed himself, Peggy Sue was more accepting and sat next to him while he ate another small snack.

Then he was ready for bed. All four of us slept together in our big king-size bed every night, and Streaker wanted to be in control of the sleeping arrangements. He usually slept with his head on my pillow and one long foreleg draped over my neck. At times this could be rather suffocating and I would push him away—which didn't upset him in the least. He simply crawled over me and hugged John around the neck!

I was learning a lot about both breeds as I watched them grow and play together. Servals are so inbred their genetics begin to fail pretty early in their lives. Streaker began to slow down rather noticeably when he turned nine. He had lost his energy and that playful spark that so defined him. I knew the end was near, but I didn't take him to the vet. Exotic cats became extremely stressed when they were crated and taken to a strange place with unpleasant hospital odors. I had lost so many pets in my life I knew there was nothing a vet could do, so I just held Streaker close and talked to him, telling him how much I loved him and it was okay to let go and walk over the rainbow bridge. I was still holding him in my arms when he took his last breath at 3:00 a.m. He was only ten years old. When I tried to lift him and carry him from the room, Peggy Sue wouldn't let me. She obviously wanted her time with him to say good-bye. I left them together, and after about an hour, she came up to me and butted her head against my leg. She knew his spirit, his soul, was gone, and she rested her head upon my knees. I buried my hands in her soft fur and held her close, crying softly. The two of us would grieve together for the next several weeks.

Chapter 14

I THREW MYSELF INTO OUR Tiger Touch Sanctuary. At that time we had seven furry residents: Teddy and Sunshine, male and female Canadian lynx; Nala, a female Barbary lion, and her mate, Rocky, also a Barbary lion; a male Bengal tiger, Det (short for Detonator); and Niki, a female Siberian tiger—and of course Peggy Sue, who lived in the house with John and me. After Rocky died, only Nala and Det were left to love and care for one another. They were all skilled in group tribal living and very comfortable with one another. They were good buddies, sharing their food and sleeping together in perfect harmony.

It was surprisingly easy to take care of all these different breeds. All they needed was love, food, and a feeling of security. My dream was to turn Tiger Touch into a learning project, to perhaps one day house a hundred big cats that needed rescuing. I knew we would need to raise a lot of money to build a compound large enough to give the cats plenty of space to roam about and—who knows?—perhaps even to breed. We realized that offering rescue and sanctuary wasn't enough; if we really wanted to help in the preservation of endangered exotic cats, we would have to expand.

In April of 1998, I read a press release from the American Museum of Natural History reporting on a nationwide survey entitled "Biodiversity in the Next Millennium" developed by the museum with Louis Harris & Associates. The results revealed that seven out of ten biologists believed we were in the midst of the largest mass extinction and the loss of species would pose a major threat to human existence in the twenty-first century. Unlike prior extinctions, the biologists believed this extinction was not a natural phenomenon but a result of human activity. That was why John and I were so passionate about protecting all big cats. We wanted to establish a safe haven for them as well as a place where we could educate and raise awareness on conservation for these rare and beautiful creatures.

In August of '96 the Catatat building was finished, and it didn't take long before it was claimed by Niki the tiger. She was extremely unhappy living outside in the compound with the other cats and let us know with a series of tiger sounds that she wanted to live indoors with people. Our recreation room was converted into Niki's room, and she was quite happy to lounge on the sofa and nap in the warmth of the fireplace. Our compound was soon full, so we moved two bobcats and a cougar next to Niki's room. They all happily shared space, and once again I marveled at how well different breeds got along together. I think it was because they all knew they were equally loved by John and me and they were safe and well cared for. All cats, domestic and wild, are hedonistic by nature; they're downright sensual in their desire for pleasure.

In February of '97, Tiger Touch was declared a nonprofit, and we all rejoiced. As the wild places shrink, the human habitat will be the only place exotic cats can survive in numbers. When I was in John's office, I could hear the soft sounds emitting from the big cats next door, their playful interacting with one another, and I smiled. In my early sixties, I felt like a grandmother to this big, rowdy group of kids who demanded my time and insisted that I stop and hug them and play with them when they wanted me to. They were like a bunch of spoiled, selfish toddlers tugging at my skirt for attention. Unfortunately, these kids would never outgrow their need for parental supervision, because civilization was so quickly encroaching on their birth homes. Each and every creature born deserves the right to live. Through no fault of their own, so many are neglected, abused, and abandoned. John and I always strongly believed that all creatures, human and animal, deserve health, joy, and contentment. As long as there is breath in my body, I will devote myself to this cause.

John has always rejected conventional wisdom. "Ban laws to remove exotic animals from cities, counties, or states are all the rage, it seems, but they are not the answer. Some people even want to reduce the number of tigers in captivity—even as their wild strongholds disappear. You can't do both and still have tigers in the world. This is madness." He was standing outside Niki's condo, and he reached out to scratch her head, which was pressed against the wire. "We need all the genetic diversity we can hold onto, not management for extinction. We need to hold the owners responsible and mandate humane treatment, but don't treat us like outlaws. Don't think that just because we love and own exotic cats we're some kind of weird rebels, thumbing our noses at the establishment." Niki butted her head against the wire and purred in agreement.

With Streaker gone, my beautiful little loner lynx transformed into a love cat. She would wait until I went to bed and then silently creep in beside me and snuggle until dawn, leaving just as quietly before I woke up. I don't know why she felt she had to sneak into bed. Maybe it was because Streaker had always set the pace for our evening slumber. He would just blunder into bed as boisterously as a big pup and settle in next to me or John, taking up his fair share of the bed. He felt that love was his specialty and would chase Peggy off the bed. Peggy Sue was a lady lynx and required her own personal space for sleeping. I placed a soft, white flannel blanket down beside me and told her this was her spot. And that's where she still sleeps to this day.

It seemed that she became calmer after Streaker passed. She was perfectly content with her family of three, which was not surprising. Triangles make for the most stable of all relationships. Feline females live in a spiritual world with simple purity. Peggy Sue started picking up my habits and time schedule. She knew what I would do from the time I woke up until I went to bed at night. I would bring a cup of coffee back to bed with me in the morning, and she would sit right beside me, inhaling the rich aroma. She wanted me to hold the cup out to her so she could really get her nose in there and smell it. She didn't drink it, of course, but she wanted to be a part of my morning ritual by smelling it. She would rub the side of her face against the rim of the mug in pure pleasure. If I didn't let her have her moment of caffeine bonding, she would swat the cup out of my hand! She loved a lot of different smells. Herbal teas were a favorite, and she was crazy about mustard. Go figure!

When she would take one of her many naps during the day, she would choose a spot in the living room where she could keep an eye on us. After dinner, we had family time in the living room, and Peggy Sue made sure to share herself with John and me equally. Sometimes she just wanted to be present but didn't want to be fooled with, and she would give a soft but firm growl, letting me know to back off for a minute. She was adamant about needing her own space. Over the years we all became tuned in to each other's needs, likes, and dislikes. When John or I wanted to be intimate with someone outside the family, it had to be completely open.

Recently, a doctor friend of mine confessed that even though she was happily married she sometimes felt sexually unfulfilled. She knew she was bisexual but didn't really get many opportunities to express herself in that way. I invited her over for a mutually satisfying evening of sex and good female conversation, and Peggy Sue was just fine with the arrangement. She leaped up on the bed and lay down next to me while my friend and I talked. The arrangement was okay, but I felt a little uneasy knowing she was lying to her husband every time she came over for sex. And truth be told, I felt kind of used. Peggy Sue apparently picked up on my vibes, because one night she just walked over and bopped her on the head! Bang! Then she chased her off the bed! My lover dressed rather hurriedly and made a hasty retreat. We're still friends but no longer lovers. I guess Peggy Sue didn't like for anyone to take advantage of her best friend—me!

For the first time since leaving Sandstone, I felt contentment. With Tiger Touch taking shape just outside in the backyard and three big cats residing in the room connected to John's office, it just felt right. I was growing my own family, in a way. I was still searching for the perfect union, and with Peggy Sue and John, I felt that maybe, at last, I had found it. I know I was more content than I had been in a long time. I awoke each morning feeling happy and eager to meet the new day, wondering what surprises might be in store for me. With big cats, you just never knew! They could be very mischievous in their play and sometimes a little rough, but I was never afraid of them. I trusted completely the gratitude I knew they felt. All of them understood that John and I had saved their lives. You could see it in their eyes and feel it in the gentle vibrations of their purrs when they butted against us and rubbed their scent glands on our clothes. They were marking us as their own.

You know, you always see these images or read stories about faithful dogs saving their masters, a perfect picture of man and dog bonding for life. In my case, it was woman and exotic cat bonding for life. The spiritual—or, more precisely, psycho-spiritual—relationship we have with animals is extremely profound. Animals show us something our human companions won't (or can't)—they give us unconditional love. This love isn't based on our good looks, or how much money we have, or what kind of career we have, or what kind of car—it's just basic, pure emotion. Their devotion is magnificent in its simplicity.

For many, many years experts in the field of human emotions have recognized the healing benefits of pairing humans with animals. They've been widely used in therapy sessions at hospitals and nursing homes. It's a proven fact that animals soothe terminal patients, giving them ease and comfort in their last days. Badly traumatized children can be coaxed out of their psychosis by bonding with a furry friend. The truly damaged among us are usually terrified of people, because people are the ones who damaged them, but they are more than willing to reach out to an animal, instinctively knowing the animal has no agenda, just love. And we all need love. It's as vital as air. Sadly, however, far too many trudge through life without love. That's always been my one clear goal—unconditional love—and I was so lucky to find it in my lifetime not just with John but with Peggy Sue as well. I feel like I won the love lottery.

I've always been fascinated by the human-animal bond and love reading accounts of the incredible acts of bravery performed by these furry creatures. We've all heard about dogs and cats alerting their people when their house caught fire or the intelligence that allows them to push the 911 button on the phone to call paramedics when their owner goes into a seizure or falls into danger in some way. I once read a remarkable story about a scrappy little Jack Russell terrier that fought off a ten-foot alligator to save his elderly owner. And a pot-bellied pig that ran into traffic, forcing cars to stop and follow him back to his house, where his owner had been felled by a heart attack. Dolphins have been celebrated since ancient times for rescuing people lost at sea, actually fighting off sharks in the process. One of the most amazing stories I read was about an African gray parrot that flew into a burning house and pecked at its owners repeatedly until they woke up and managed to escape. The parrot suffered major feather loss, and his feet were badly blistered, but he didn't give up until his people were safe. If that isn't love, I don't know what love is!

We all know that dogs have always been trained as guides for the blind and helpers for the disabled, fetching items, opening doors, and alerting them to any possible danger; but I saw a story on Animal Planet just recently that truly amazed me about a seeing-eye miniature horse! Smaller than a great dane, this little pony confidently guided his owner down the sidewalk and in and out of stores, halting at street corners and giving a gentle nudge when it was safe to cross the street. Amazing!

Over the years I've been very intrigued by the use of capuchin monkeys to aid paraplegics. These tiny little fur-people can use a computer, insert tapes and DVDs, answer phones, fetch items, open cans of soda, wipe up spills—in short, they can do almost anything you and I can do. And they form a strong, protective bond with their humans, loving them unconditionally. They see their humans as their mates, their families, and they will fight to the death to secure that family unit. Which proves that we all—human and animal alike—need a loving partner in life. I have been so very blessed to have experienced both kinds of love, and you know something? They're pretty much the same. They both fill your heart so full the love overflows and touches every part of your being.

Tiger Touch

Chapter 15

IT WAS COMING CLOSE TO the end of the twentieth century. I was happily retired and completely engrossed in the growth of Tiger Touch. In retrospect, what a foolhardy and potentially dangerous career move! I had never had a bit of formal training about how to deal with very large exotic felines, especially felines who came from abusive backgrounds and had every right to hate all humans! I just blundered ahead with my arms open and my heart filled with compassion for those frightened, damaged kitties. I always looked at them as if they were just kitties—a hell of lot bigger, for sure, but under all those muscles and fur was still a cat not unlike your own tabby sleeping by the hearth.

As mentioned earlier in this book, I got my first exotic cat in 1971—PC, or Pusser, as he came to be called. He lived in the motor home with John and me from day one and clearly saw himself as an ambassador from the wild. He taught us the concept of Gaia, the web of life that binds us all together. He instilled in us stewardship, a notion that humankind seems to have lost somewhere along the way. He lived by his own set of principles, his values of truth, love, and dignity. There's a certain regal look and feel of royalty, a mantle that all exotic breeds wear as casually as an old bathrobe. He lived for twenty years, unheard of for a bobcat in captivity, but then he was never a captive—maybe that's the difference. He was a member of a loving family unit.

We don't know anything about Buffy, a male bobcat that wandered into our lives shortly after Pusser died. He looked healthy and well cared for, so we suspected he'd somehow gotten lost or separated from his people and found us. He had a strong personality and always radiated sweetness and joy. He was very gregarious and often invited raccoons, skunks, squirrels, and other creatures into the house to share his dinner! We never caged him, because he wasn't a wild animal. He was a family member and shared our bed and board as comfortably as a poodle might. We only had him for a couple of years, and then he quietly passed away in his sleep, leaving us as mysteriously as he had found us.

Of all the big cats we nurtured and loved at Tiger Touch, Satchel was one who tugged at my heart. He was a big, handsome cougar, weighing in at two hundred and twenty-five pounds. He suffered from diabetes and was badly crippled from a botched declawing and, I suspect, some physical abuse. But he never lost his dignity or the ability to love. He embraced everyone with a deep, rolling purr and the expectation of having his love returned. At Tiger Touch it was returned tenfold. Everyone who ever met him mourned his passing. I sometimes see him now running wild and free, moving with the feline grace that he didn't have here on earth, and I applaud his strong spirit and forgiving heart.

Aptly named Leroy Brown, one feisty little lynx loved to sing! He would make up lyrics and sing them long and loud. At first I thought he was caterwauling to get out of the Catatat where he was housed with a few other cats, but no—he was singing! You could hear a sort of melodic joy in his voice, and sometimes he would actually imitate sounds from around the yard. There was something soothing about the tone of his voice, as if he knew and appreciated that he had been rescued and now had a forever home. And he was quite happy indeed when we paired him with a female lynx, Passion, who sashayed into the yard and stole his heart.

Passion was a saucy little female with major attitude. She was not a cuddle cat, and it was considered a capital offense to even think about petting her. And if you were foolish enough to try it, you might lose a finger! However, she too realized and understood that she was safe at last and at Tiger Touch she would get food, shelter, and a cute boyfriend. I was the only human she warmed up to, and she would tolerate me in the cage in her own aloof way. She never lost her antisocial attitude, but she was content and well cared for.

After a few months of dealing with all the rescue cats and the pain and ill treatment they had endured, my heart was aching and felt battered. I longed for a companion cat, someone who had never known pain or hardship, a cat who hadn't learned to be wary of humans. I found her in 1996 when I took a little five-week-old bundle of joy home with me. Peggy Sue was the answer to my dreams. She is a Eurasian lynx, (sometimes called a Siberian lynx), the largest of the lynx subspecies indigenous to much of northern Europe, Russia, and central Asia. Having known nothing but love since the moment she was born, Peggy Sue is gentle, kindhearted and compassionate. (Yes, animals do feel and show compassion for those they love.) In the wild, the Eurasian lynx feeds on deer and other small game, but Peggy Sue has developed a more sophisticated, civilized palette—a taste for coffee in the morning, cantaloupe, bananas, tuna, Zu-Preem with an algae supplement, and pretty much whatever she finds tasty. She is that very rare of all cat breeds—a cuddle companion. She's the perfect example of how humans and animals can not only coexist and become best friends but benefit from each other as well. At sixty pounds, she's a big girl, but in her heart she's still a lap cub and wants her cuddles. She's seventeen years old as of the writing of this book, and I don't even let myself think about her ever leaving me.

John's favorites were always the cougars, so you can imagine his joy when we received two females, sisters Kicky and Missy, at Tiger Touch. Kicky was one cool cat, so named because she loved to just kick back and sun herself. Her beautiful blond fur was as luxurious as a mink coat. Perhaps the only breed of exotic cats to be called by a variety of names—cougar, puma, panther, painter, mountain lion—they are always beautiful. With eyes the color of warm gold, their coats range from a golden blond to a deep dusky tan, their extraordinarily long tails black tipped and strong enough to knock a full-grown gazelle off its feet. They can be found over much of the United States and Canada and are on the endangered list. Missy was definitely a girly girl; affectionate and loving, gentle and kindhearted, she loved to be petted and hugged. Her loud purr rumbled throughout her body, and when she leaned against me I had to brace myself so I wouldn't topple over. They both came to us in 1995, sort of cofounders of Tiger Touch, and sweet Missy took that last, long walk over the rainbow bridge in 2005, followed four years later by Kicky in 2009. They are both still sorely missed.

Teddy, a shy Canadian lynx, never quite came out of his shell. Leery of people, he retreated to his den box at the sight of someone approaching the compound. We never found out much about his background—only that he had been abused and abandoned, but that's really all we needed to know to open our doors and heart to him. Much smaller than a Eurasian lynx, Teddy weighed in at twenty-five pounds. Teddy had beautiful markings. His large eyes were outlined in black, giving him a Cleopatra look, and his ears were also rimmed in black with wonderful tufts on the tips. His cheek tufts were thick and luxurious. I loved his huge paws. They were as big as a dinner plate and as soft as the finest velvet. I thought the size of those paws must surely be a hindrance until John told me the paws served as snowshoes in the deep snow of Canada, enabling the lynx to move swiftly over the surface without breaking through.

Sunshine is also a Canadian lynx. She's a shy little girl at just twenty-five pounds, smaller than a lot of dog breeds. She used to spend all her time with Teddy hanging out in their den and watching the goings on around them. Teddy passed away in 2012, and Sunshine is still with us, the only exotic left at Tiger Touch besides Peggy Sue.

Rocky was our first Barbary lion, a big, imposing male, 450 pounds with a full dark mane and whiskers at least a foot long. He was everything a lion should be—regal, dignified, proud, and magnificent in every way.

One expected him to be wearing a robe of purple satin and a crown of jewels! He was the king of beasts, the king of cool. He had suffered so much physical and emotional abuse before he came to us, I wouldn't have blamed him if he had tried to kill us all. But like a wise old king, he realized we were friends, not foes. He gratefully accepted the shelter and responded to our offered love with his mighty head held high and proud. How he could still do that after suffering so much pain is beyond me. I guess it just goes to show class is something you're born with. For all the gratitude Rocky felt, I felt twice as much, because I was able to give him all the love and support he so richly deserved during his last fifteen years on earth. I can see him now, reigning supreme in that great litter box in the sky, gently lording it over a harem of adoring females.

Nala was just one of the females who adored him. Also a Barbary lion, she was larger at five hundred pounds but every bit as regal. Her coat was the color of honey, and she swaggered with an arrogant stride about the compound, swishing her long tail. She was a practical joker and loved to surprise Rocky and their roommate, Det the Bengal tiger. Nala was every inch the queen. John and I often laughingly called her "your majesty," and she would nod her massive head in acknowledgement. But for all her royal demeanor, she was a playful prankster at heart. She delighted in lying in wait for someone to walk by and then pouncing at the fence before they knew what happened. We had some huge wooden reels in the compound weighing close to a hundred pounds, and Nala would swat them all over the place as easily as a domestic tabby would swat a tennis ball. Barbary lions were once prevalent throughout northern Africa but now are almost extinct, with only a handful still living in zoos. John and I wanted to breed Nala and Rocky, but even though they were constant companions, they did not make me a grandma!

Niki, our Siberian tiger, passed away only last year, and the wound is still fresh in my heart. She was a big girl at 420 pounds and as gentle as a kitten. Siberian tigers are the largest of all exotic breeds, averaging about 700 pounds and measuring fourteen feet from nose to tail. Sadly, the Siberian tiger is among the most critically endangered. Where once they roamed most of northeast Asia, there are now less than two hundred living in the wild and about five hundred residing in zoos and sanctuaries. Niki was a people tiger, enjoying the company of her humans and letting us know in no uncertain terms that she wanted to live with us, not in some outdoor compound like a common cat. Obviously, we couldn't let her into the house with us; 420 pounds of pussycat was a little too much pussy! And we had Peggy Sue to consider. So John turned part of the Catatat into private, air-conditioned quarters for Miss Niki. The bedroom was fourteen feet by twelve feet with an elevated walkway and a bench for lounging. Her playroom was forty-five feet by twelve feet and opened outside to a large all-weather deck. Did I mention that she also had a small swimming pool? (I know. I know. I spoil my babies rotten.) Niki's quarters were on the other side of the wall to John's office, so people were constantly walking by her enclosure, and she loved it. Her curiosity never waned in all the years she lived. She would lie dozing on her bench listening to music, waiting to visit with whoever might stop by for a chat. When friends came to visit John and me, Niki thought they were her guests and would greet them with a series of soft snuffles, a sort of combination of purrs and snores. All big cats have a unique way of talking, and after so many years spent with them I prided myself on speaking Felinese.

The Detonator (Det for short) lived up to his name. He was the largest cat at Tiger Touch, weighing in at six hundred pounds and measuring nine feet from nose to tail tip. A magnificent, handsome Bengal tiger, he was strong and smart and strutted his stuff with regal self-confidence. To the females in the compound (and one male, Rocky the lion) he was six hundred pounds of catnip! His markings were incredibly beautiful—jet black stripes on a background of honey-hued orange fur. Each tiger has its own unique stripe pattern, and no two are the same—kind of like a person's fingerprints. Because tigers are the most seriously endangered of all the big cats, we so hoped and prayed that Det and Niki would breed and give us at least one little cub, but it wasn't to be.

For all his lordly ways, Det must surely have been a little rattled when John (upon first meeting) casually stuck his head into Det's mouth! And yes, Det's mouth when fully open could easily encircle John's head! There was a kind of "Huh?" moment and then John withdrew his head, patted Det on his massive shoulder, and sauntered away. Det sat staring after him for a long moment with just the tip of his tail switching, his yellow eyes following John as he moved about tending to the other cats. That was it. They were best buddies for the next fifteen years, enjoying a bond of trust and friendship that never wavered.

When we first started Tiger Touch and began receiving big cats, we kept them in separate quarters with heavy latches on the doors. They all wore heavy collars that allowed us to grasp them in a controlling hold if need be, and they all stayed in their own cages, released into the big compound only for daily exercise. It didn't take long for them to let us know they weren't happy with that arrangement; they all wanted to be free and enjoy the space outside rather than be kept in cages. By this time I figured they were used to each other's scent, so we removed their collars, opened the gates, and let them have free roaming space. There were a few little scuffles; long, glowering stares; and a lot of hissing and empty threats (much like school boys on the playground) but soon they all settled into their new home and learned to live with this odd set of roommates. All felines, large or small, prefer to live in groups (or prides) and share a love and dependency just like humans. Feline brothers and sisters who grow up together, sharing the same teat, as it were, have a closeness that is broken only by death. You always hear that old adage that "elephants never forget"—well, felines don't, either. There have been numerous documented cases in which a lion (or other cat) raised by humans and then separated for whatever reason instantly remembers its humans when reunited. The joy and love these cats show register on their faces as brightly as a neon sign. It makes me livid when scoffers say, "Aw, they're just animals. They don't have emotions like we do."

My only response is, "You ignorant fool!"

Rocky the lion most certainly had human emotions. He didn't like sleeping alone, and although I constantly tried to push him in the direction of Nala the lioness, he preferred the company of our dog, a large male mastiff. He used him as a pillow and also tried to hump him on a regular basis! *This is very interesting,* I remember thinking. *Do we have the only gay lion in captivity?* Rocky's homosexual tendencies blossomed when he met the handsome and macho Det and pursued him as avidly as a lovesick schoolboy with his first crush. He would ease himself onto Det's back and take a mouthful of skin and fur just between his shoulder blades, the accepted way cats mate, but before he could make entry, Det would easily roll him off. Then they would engage in a sort of halfhearted wrestling match with Rocky taking a submissive position as if to say, "Hey, man, I was just kidding! I wasn't really trying to fuck you!"

Seeing the rough play, the dog would become protective of Rocky and bark like crazy, taking on a pretend bravado and rushing in to nip at Det's rear end. He was clearly jealous, but Det was not impressed. He let us know that if we didn't get rid of the dog, he would! So we moved the mastiff to a safer area, and a crisis was averted. However, this in no way diminished Rocky's ardor, and he continued to try to hump Det every chance he got. In spite of the unrequited love affair, Det and Rocky became fast friends and spent all their time together. They played and napped together, shared their meals, and slept with their limbs entwined. And Rocky doggedly continued to pursue Det even as Det continued to rebuff him. It was a strange relationship but one that seemed to work for them.

Nala was only five months old when we got her, and even though we tried like crazy to get her interested in Rocky, she preferred Det. Nala still had a lot of kitten play in her, and Det matched her energy and curiosity, always up for a good romp around the compound. Several times Rocky and Det got into it, wrestling around, roaring, and growling like they were going to kill each other, but I could clearly see it was all just fake fighting. Their claws were still safely sheathed, and their huge, four-inch-long fangs never penetrated. It was definitely a jealousy thing, and if it had been two males in the jungle going at it over a female, it would have been perfectly normal. But Rocky was jealous of the time Det spent playing with Nala instead of with him! And then there was the mastiff on the other side of fence, pissed off at Det because he could no longer spend time with his buddy, Rocky. See? Even in the animal kingdom, jealousy rears its ugly head …

Nala had a second love that was as dear to her as Det. She was crazy about John. After careful observation, it was apparent she was just a little embarrassed to love a human as much as she loved John, and she developed sneaky little ways of showing him her adoration. She would sidle up to him and butt her head against his leg and then push her big nose into his hand. She would follow him while he was doing chores, sitting patiently about two feet away and watching him and then following him when he moved on to another chore. The exception was when John took power tools into the compound to do repairs. Nala would steal them away. There was no doubt in her mind she was the most competent engineer, and she felt she could better fix what was broken. It took her a long time to warm up to me, but when she finally did it was a wonderful bond. She and Rocky would often stand together on a small knoll in the compound and roar at the sky just for the love of it. John joined in, roaring almost as loudly as they did. Both massive heads swung in his direction with looks of astonishment, and I was just standing there laughing. It was great theater! It became a ritual whenever there was a full moon—John and the two lions roaring at the moon. I reminded him that howling at the moon was something reserved for wolves. "They're howling," said John, grinning. "We're roaring!" The roars were heard as far as fifteen miles away.

Nala also formed a very close, loving bond with Kicky the cougar. They played together and napped with their paws flopped over each other's back, faces close together. No one believed us until they saw for themselves so many different species coexisting peacefully and sharing real affection. Lions, tigers, bobcats, cougars, and lynx—it was truly remarkable.

Chapter 16

I WAS NOW CONTENT. EARLY in the twenty-first century, I felt I had finally found my passion and niche in life. I had always believed that the power of love was the strongest emotion on earth, and I had proved this to be true first with the free love of Sandstone and now with a compound of many different species of exotic cats all living and loving in harmony. In the wild, these natural enemies would have instinctively killed each other, but here at Tiger Touch love overrode hate and fear. In order to love, you must first trust, and I can honestly say that each and every cat trusted us. I had my big, loving family at last.

Through the years, magazine articles often called me "the most liberated woman in America," a fearless, courageous woman who threw herself wholeheartedly into the quest for an alternative lifestyle, a woman unafraid to say she wanted to change the world. I did change my own world, traveling down a challenging path of self-discovery through social engineering. When I cofounded Sandstone, I created an environment that allowed others to explore and enjoy an alternate lifestyle. Very few women in history have ever attempted to go up against the cultural edicts as I did. I am very proud of that.

Perhaps Sandstone didn't change the world in the way I hoped it would, but I put the vibes out there in the universe, and who knows what the future holds? I've been asked, "Are you a visionary?" and I don't really know. Maybe I am. I know from a very early age I always knew I wanted to be surrounded by love; that's all—just love, acceptance, security, and peace. I found that with John, my soul mate, my lover to the very end of time. I found the same unconditional love from the big cats I was lucky enough to have in my world. But the one thing I hadn't thought about was how to say good-bye when they left my world.

The first and most painful loss was, of course, my sweet little Pusser, my bobcat PC, who passed away in 1991 after spending his entire life of twenty years with me. He was followed in '94 by Buffy, leaving me filled with dread and pain, praying for the health and longevity of all future cats we might have. And we were very lucky, because many years would pass before any more family members took that last, long walk across the rainbow bridge. My sweet little girl Missy the cougar was the next one to go, leaving us in 2005 and followed two years later by the singing bobcat, Leroy Brown. Two more years would pass before Kicky joined her sister, Missy, and I thought John's heart would break. The two female cougars were always John's girls, and he took their loss very hard.

By this time we had a cemetery where we buried our little family, and every time I passed it, I was filled with the anguish of loss. But then I would calm myself, knowing that they would not have lived another week unless we had rescued them, and I thanked God for all the wonderful years they had filled my heart with love.

Rocky was the next to go, passing away quietly in his sleep in the fall of 2010, and I just knew he was strong and whole again, romping through the clouds with his good buddies Satchel, Kicky, and Missy. He left behind two old friends that grieved for him for a long time, Det and Nala. They would pace the enclosure, pawing at the blanket he had slept on, rolling in the same places he had rolled and played. Sometimes they would lie side by side, their heads close together, their expressions filled with grief and loss. After watching those two cats mourn the loss of their friend, no one can ever tell me lions and tigers do not have feelings of love and loss. I saw it and felt it.

Exactly a year later, in the fall of 2011, Nala joined Rocky and the others in that special paradise that God holds just for the most deserving of his creatures. I comforted myself with that knowledge, knowing that Nala would be met by all her old pals, who would show her the ropes in that new place. I was so glad I had been able to give her peace and love in the last fifteen years of her life. What a blessing Tiger Touch had been to all those abandoned, neglected, and abused throwaways who would surely have died without John's dedication and physical labor. It was damn hard work keeping a huge place like Tiger Touch running, keeping it clean, keeping fences and housing repaired and comfortable. John was most assuredly an angel sent down to earth with a smile on his face and a message to spread the love wherever it was needed.

We now had only four beautiful cats in our life—Niki, the female Siberian tiger; Det, the Bengal; Sunshine, the Canadian lynx; and, of course, our love cat, Peggy Sue. We were all getting a little older and a little slower. Life itself had slowed down considerably for all of us. I turned seventy-three in April of 2012, and the deaths of Niki and Det were like bookends at that troubled time. Niki passed in February, and Det followed in May. It was a double whammy straight to my heart. John held me and soothed me with words I knew to be true—they were both really old, especially for exotic cats in captivity; they had had the best care and the deepest love possible for more than fifteen years; they had been free to run and play and share their lives with others of their kind. It was just their time to go as all of us must.

Now the shy little Canadian lynx, Sunshine, lived alone in her little compound. I named her Sunshine as a sort of joke because she was just the opposite. Leery of all humans, she spent much of her time hiding in her box and would only come out to socialize with the others when she was damn sure no humans were lurking about. She was the youngest of our cats and the smallest at just twenty-five pounds. She was now eleven years old and in good health. I guess she soon realized I was all she had left, and she finally started to warm up to me, allowing me into her cage without the usual hissing that had greeted me before. John and I sort of kicked around the idea of trying to find a companion for her, but we too were getting up there and just were not sure we still had the physical strength. Looking after animals that size is quite a challenge!

Of course we still had our darling Peggy Sue, who was not a chore but a blessing. I can sincerely say that after all our years together she has become a sort of daughter and best friend. She's seventeen years old now and, thanks to the Lord, in good health.

Sadly and shockingly, John's health suddenly began to fail. I was indeed shaken to my core, shocked and disbelieving. John was my rock. He was invincible. He was my savior and my saint. Saviors didn't get sick; they healed the sick. He had healed me by whisking me away on his magic carpet of unconditional love. Where would my life have been if he had not found and married me and changed my world? He had opened my eyes to all sorts of possibilities and introduced me to a world of experiences that I otherwise would never have known. He was the wind beneath my wings. He had allowed me space and freedom to soar as high as I could and still kept me tethered to him by his unconditional love. No one had ever loved me so completely.

I'm not going to go into all the doctor appointments and hospital trips, the different diagnoses and medications, the frustration of not knowing exactly what was wrong with John. Suffice it to say his health was rapidly failing. More than once he was admitted to the hospital, and I was told to prepare myself for the inevitable—he might not be going home with me. But each time he rallied, astonishing the doctors and thrilling me with his will to live.

Then, the first week in March 2013, we were told he was suffering from complications due to lung cancer. I couldn't believe it. We had both stopped smoking cigarettes in the midseventies. It broke my heart to see this gentle giant of a man lying in a hospital bed with all the tubes, IV bags, and paraphernalia—but I also had to smile each time I walked into his room. There was always a gaggle of nurses surrounding his bed, teasing him, flirting, listening to his stories—he was still the messiah of sex!

My darling life companion quietly passed away at 8:40 p.m. on March 24, 2013. I just went numb. My body went into automatic pilot mode—I got up, drank coffee, dressed, and moved about the house slowly taking care of business. Every time I took Peggy Sue into my arms to hug her, I couldn't stop the tears. I soaked her fur with my sorrow, and she grieved with me, missing John as much as I did. She became so lethargic that I feared I might lose her as well. I knew it was quite possible for animals to die of a broken heart, so I lavished her with love, assuring her that we still had each other.

John's daughter, Sheila Ellington, who lives in Washington, immediately drove to Nevada to take over. What a wonderful blessing! She handled all the details that I just couldn't wrap my mind around. We both knew that an ordinary funeral for such an extraordinary man was out of the question. John was too spiritual, too special to be laid to rest in a cemetery full of strangers. He loved nature and freedom and open skies—and he loved the unique. We found this park in the desert called the Gardens, a place for natural burials. His casket was a simple one made entirely of biodegradable seaweed and festooned with gorgeous yellow flowers. The headstone is a large rock with his name and the dates painted on the front. My name is also painted there for the time when I will once again lie beside him. The grounds are serene, and there's a lovely apple tree with a bench beneath it where I can sit when I go for visits.

Sheila stayed with me for one week, and each day we told stories about John and cried and laughed and remembered. On especially tough nights, Sheila would crawl into bed with Peggy Sue and me, and the three of us would fall into troubled sleep. I can't even imagine any other woman who would share her bed with a large Siberian lynx in order to comfort her stepmother! Sheila, my dear, you are a remarkable woman.

After Sheila left, I faced the difficult task of e-mailing friends with the news of John's passing. My God! I was stunned by the response! I was deluged with e-mails from all over the world not just from close friends but from mere acquaintances or from strangers who had only heard about or read about John. Everyone expressed their admiration for John's boldness when he created Sandstone. Those who had actually visited Sandstone said their experience there had changed their lives for the better, and those who had never been there said it was something they would always regret.

I did not send out a press release about John's passing because, after all, Sandstone had happened more than four decades ago, and I wasn't sure anyone would even remember. Oh boy, was I ever wrong! John was widely lauded as the king of the sexual revolution, the messiah of sex. On May 4, the *New York Times* published this tribute to him:

John and Barbara Williamson always insisted that Sandstone Retreat was about more than sex. By all means, help yourself to each other, they would say. But the goal was larger than spouse-swapping or fulfilling forbidden lust. They said that their fifteen unconventionally inhabited acres in the Topanga Canyon area near Los Angeles, formally known as the Sandstone Foundation for Community Systems Research, was about understanding society—and setting it free.

"We believe in the sexual self as being at the core of organized sexual behavior," Mr. Williamson told the Los Angeles Times in 1972, three years after Sandstone was formed. "When sexuality is distorted, it leads to a distortion of the basic self."

Mr. Williamson, whose death on March 24 in Reno, Nevada, was not widely reported, had spent most of the last two decades running a nonprofit sanctuary for tigers and other big cats rescued from neglect or abandonment. Mr. Williamson was 80, more than four decades removed from his bold moment at the forefront of the sexual revolution.

At the peak of its popularity, Sandstone had a handful of couples who were full-time residents and about 500 paying members ($240 to join, then $15 per month), with a wide range of prominent names among them, including Daniel Ellsberg, who leaked the Pentagon Papers, and the singer Bobby Darin. But it was a journalist who put it on the cultural map.

"He walked in the building and said, 'I'm Gay Talese, I'm a writer from New York, and I'm here to write a book about you,'" Marty Zitter, one of Sandstone's earliest members, said in an interview on Tuesday, recalling the day Mr. Talese arrived in 1971. "I said, 'Take a number.'"

The book, Thy Neighbor's Wife, an examination of America's changing sexual culture, became a best seller when it was published in 1980. By then—Mr. Talese spent nine years researching and writing, including considerable time experiencing Sandstone in the flesh—the retreat had closed, in part because of financial problems, and the Williamsons had re-entered the clothed confines of mainstream society.

"We merged back into the culture that we disliked so much," Mrs. Williamson said in an interview on Tuesday.

John Decatur Williamson was born on July 31, 1932, near Mobile, Ala. He grew up poor, joined the navy at 17 and was soon traveling the world, spending time in California and the South Pacific. He learned electrical engineering in the service and in the late 1950s worked on the Polaris missile project in Cape Canaveral, Fla.

He returned to California and in 1966, met Barbara Cramer, an insurance saleswoman who was making her pitch to the electronics firm he was managing.

They soon found they shared an interest in psychology, including studies by Abraham Maslow that emphasized the possibility of achieving 'self-actualization' through the sequential fulfillment of basic needs. Five weeks later, they married while double-parked outside the courthouse in Las Vegas.

They had immediately known they were meant for each other, Mrs. Williamson said, and for others. 'We just knew that a traditional heterosexual marriage could not last, because two people could not give each other everything they needed,' she said. 'So we built a bigger marriage.'

They built it at Sandstone. Upstairs, people would lounge and talk—some naked, some not—in a room with gold-colored shag carpet, a huge fireplace and vast views of the canyon. Downstairs was known as the Ballroom.

"It was like the Algonquin," Mr. Zitter said of the upper floor. "Then people would go downstairs and have sex, and then they'd come back upstairs and talk some more. Some people," he added, "wanted to have sex right there in the conversation."

Mr. Talese listened and watched and participated.

"Like the founding fathers of other utopian settlements in the past, he was unhappy with the world around him," he wrote of Mr. Williamson. "He regarded contemporary life in America as destructive to the spirit, organized religion as a celestial swindle, the federal government as cumbersome and avaricious; he saw the average wage earner, who was excessively taxed and easily replaced, as existing only with detached participation in a computerized society."

Mr. Talese sold film rights for his book for $2.5 million, a starling amount, and though it was never made into a movie, the Williamsons and another couple received payments of $50,000.00.

In an interview on Thursday, Mr. Talese said one of Mr. Williamson's central ambitions was for people to be honest about their personal and sexual lives and not be embarrassed about it.

"It wasn't really about sex, because they got beyond the sex to the stage where they didn't have to lie about anything."

Mr. Williamson died of cancer, Mrs. Williamson said. Other survivors include a daughter from a previous marriage and a granddaughter. A son from his first marriage died in a drowning accident when he was five.

The Williamsons had sold Sandstone by early 1973. They had tried but failed to raise money to start a much larger "growth center" in Montana that was to include 1,000 residents. Scientists and theologians were to be invited and everyone would live in geodesic domes linked by enclosed walkways to protect naked residents from the cold.

Mr. Williamson eventually returned to a career in electronics, and Mrs. Williamson to insurance. They lived in the San Francisco area and, Mrs. Williamson said, "had some great parties." Their open-marriage policy ended in 1995, the year they moved to Nevada to devote themselves to the big cats.

"They just really gave us a lot of satisfaction," Mrs. Williamson said.

Even though I was surprised and flattered that the *New York Times* would devote so much space to us, I was also a little disappointed. The article was rather simplistic and didn't really explain the passion and dedication John and I felt about an alternative lifestyle. Sandstone was the epitome of the sexual revolution. It was a brave and ballsy experiment that actually worked. We had single-handedly brought together groups of strangers to live in peace and harmony, to put aside jealousy and possessiveness, to share everything from food to sex without embarrassment or resentment. Unfortunately, as our membership grew so did the costs. It became impossible for just a small handful of people (the live-in members) to keep the place clean, buy supplies, and provide the kind of setting that John and I knew we had to have in order to succeed. We had never charged enough for membership, because we didn't want Sandstone to be about money. Of course that became impossible. Much to our disgust, everything is about money. Once the free-wheeling days of the hippie generation began to wane, so did everything else. As Bob Dylan put it, "My friend, the times they are a-changing ..."

Well, we didn't want to change. We wanted Sandstone to remain pure and simple, a place of serenity where everyone could just be—a place completely free of artificiality. And we had it for a time. Every so often when I think about those days it reminds me of that famous line from the musical Camelot: "For one brief and shining moment, there was Camelot ..."

Maybe I romanticized it—I don't know—but in my memories, Sandstone was like Camelot with the wise and benevolent King Arthur (John) reigning over a peaceful kingdom based on love and acceptance, a land where there was no war or greed or coveting. I used to think that maybe I was the only one who felt that way, but after John died and e-mails and phone calls poured in from around the world, I finally realized that we had indeed touched a generation. The Internet exploded with tributes to him—to us, really—and it filled my heart to overflowing. Obviously, the tributes were too numerous to reprint here, but there's one I want to share with you that was posted by Neil Strauss:

In Memory of a Sexual Freedom Fighter

On March 24th at 8:40 p.m., John Williamson, one of the leading figures of the Sexual Revolution (and a forerunner of the sex-positive movement today) passed away from complications due to lung cancer. Williamson was best known for creating the legendary Sandstone Retreat in Los Angeles with his wife, Barbara.

"He wanted everybody to be human beings—with an emphasis on being," Barbara recalled. "He liked the idea of being a sexual Messiah. He was bringing a message of cooperation, pleasure and freedom. And people weren't necessarily listening."

In 1968, Williamson purchased a secluded decaying 15 acre estate nestled in the Topanga Canyon hills overlooking Malibu. He had a vision of creating a utopian experiment in which men and women lived together in sexual freedom and equality, free of possessiveness and jealousy. So he began to gather like-minded couples who shared his disappointment with the current system, lack of meaning in the rat race, and tedium of common jobs and marriages. In 1969, that renovated property became the Sandstone Foundation for Community Systems Research, a not-for-profit organization more commonly known as the Sandstone Retreat. As she puts it in the manuscript of a memoir Barbara is currently completing, it was created as a "retreat from artificiality … designed to promote human relations at all levels."

"I don't know a person who came to Sandstone and forgot it," Barbara said. "It was the highlight of their lives. It was the highlight of mine, too, and it always will be."

The intentional community and its philosophy that the human body and open expressions of affection and sexuality should not be sources of shame soon became a mecca for everyone from film stars to anthropologists to rockers to factory workers to professors. As Barbara puts it in her unfinished memoir-in-progress, "I can honestly say I saw more naked stars than any other woman in Hollywood!" Though it had its fair share of struggles, Sandstone never fell prey to the excessive megalomania, in-fighting, disorganization, drug abuse, control, and fissures that tarnished the reputation of many other free-love communities of the time, making it living proof that the free-love ideas espoused in science fiction novels by Robert Heinlein and Robert Rimmer could work in reality. "Bob Rimmer is one of the people who coined the phrase that John was the Messiah of Sex," Barbara recalled when we spoke. "We had a good time with him, but all our friends are dead now."

John Williamson was born in 1932 in the swamplands of Alabama to Claude and Constance Williamson. His father was a hunter, fisherman and moonshine-bootlegger who had lost his left arm trying to climb on a moving freight train; his mother was an introverted, studious woman who loved books.

His family lived in primitive conditions in a communal environment. It was a nameless place of woodlands, log cabins, and clannish families who came together and helped each other with procuring food, building and maintaining shelter, doing chores, raising children. John's first sexual experience was at the age of 12 with a slightly older cousin.

In 1949, John enlisted in the Navy and was briefly sent as an electronics technician to the American occupational forces in the South Pacific. In 1953, while working as a civilian government employee, he married an aspiring German anthropologist named Lilo Goetz and they moved to Florida so he could work for Boeing at Cape Canaveral. In 1957 he began working on missile support systems for Lockheed.

A series of tragedies—including the accidental drowning of their five-year-old son and the loss of a big government assignment after Russians shot down the U-2 spy plane he'd been working on—led to a period of bitterness and heavy drinking for Williamson.

In late 1962, however, he discovered the novel *Atlas Shrugged* by Ayn Rand and developed a new outlook on life. He suddenly understood, among other things, that the type of life he'd been looking for could not be found, but he could create it. So he resigned his position at Cape Canaveral and moved to Los Angeles with his wife and surviving daughter. They divorced a year later.

In 1966, when he was managing an electronics firm, John met Barbara Cramer when she attempted to sell him an insurance policy. Five weeks later, they got married in Las Vegas.

John's career ambitions began shifting from mechanical engineering to concerns for contemporary society and more esoteric topics, and he became interested in the work of Austrian psychiatrist Wilhelm Reich, who, among other things, believed that repressing emotional and sexual expression walled people off from happiness, connection, and ultimately life. Inspired by Reich and the human potential workshops at places like the Esalen Institute in Big Sur, John decided to establish a community for couples where there could be an atmosphere that was sexually open and free from jealousy, guilt, double standards, possessiveness, and lies.

In 1968, John resigned from his electronics firm, sold his company stock, and beat out pop group the Monkeys to purchase the Topanga Canyon estate that would become the Sandstone Retreat.

Sandstone was perceived by some as a sex club or swingers' retreat, but for John and Barbara it was much more than that, an alternative lifestyle community and sociological research center. As Barbara put it, "Sandstone was a university where people could learn to relate."

At its peak, there were 14 full-time residents, including the Williamsons, more than five hundred members, and a variety of facilities, all of which were clothing -optional. When describing Sandstone's lifestyle and objectives, John Williamson said, "We believe in the sexual self as being the core of organized social behavior. When sexuality is distorted, it leads to a distortion of the basic self." It wasn't uncommon for visitors to see couples in various configurations embracing the pool, or in exploring each other in various configurations on the mattresses in the downstairs "Ballroom"—its name derived from the slang term for intercourse—"balling." "The nice thing about Sandstone is we looked at sex as being so positive, and we gave everyone permission," said Barbara. "We believed that the body and the mind were pretty good. And people should be free to experience an alternative lifestyle, and it unleashed some shackles. And all of a sudden, sex was pretty nice."

Contrary to what many detractors in the community tried to say, this kind of liberation didn't damage their marriage. "Since we each had the freedom to enjoy people sexually and otherwise, it didn't put any strain on our marriage," Barbara said. "Our motto is: If we wanted to have a good marriage, we had to have a bigger one. And we lasted for forty-seven years."

Sandstone was financed by its club members, who paid a $240 a year membership, allowing them to come to the retreat and use the facilities whenever they desired. Every weekend hundreds of couples would come to copulate with strangers, participate in group sex, swap partners, and revel in natural beauty, complete sexual freedom, and a communal, tribal environment. During the day there was clothing-optional swimming, sunbathing, reading, chess, and nature walks. At night there were gourmet buffets, soft rock music, progressive discourse on the couches around the large fireplace—and orgies downstairs in the Playroom and Ballroom.

The Sandstone Retreat was a historical part of the sexual revolution of the 60's and 70's and was written about extensively in the bestseller *Thy Neighbor's Wife* by Gay Talese, in *Hot and Cool Sex* by Robert Francoeur, and in the 1973 edition of *More Joy of Sex* by Dr. Alex Comfort, among many others. All of these writers, of course, spent a lot of time enjoying research at Sandstone. It was also the subject of a 1975 documentary called *Sandstone*.

In 1973, John and Barbara Williamson decided to close Sandstone Retreat and set their sights on an even bigger project to influence the culture.

They'd planned to sell the Retreat to an alcohol addiction recovery center, but the Santa Monica Mountains were rezoned, and businesses were no longer allowed to operate there. Eventually, Sandstone reopened in 1974 under the ownership of former members before closing for good at the end of 1976 due to financial difficulties. The property is now owned and operated by a family that makes its money in land development.

Leaving Los Angeles, Barbara and John went to the wilderness of Montana along with a young chef from Sandstone. "We hoped to build a tribal community up there to improve humanity and help make the world a better place," Barbara recalled. "We planned salons with all the most beautiful scientists and religious leaders, where we'd discuss planning the future and steering the culture in the best direction."

But this site of Project Synergy, as they called the isolated community for some one hundred people they were building, was abandoned after the Federal government claimed the land, preventing any further building on the property. The following years were spent in a search for funding to take what they'd learned at Sandstone to the next level.

"The next step for us would be to have a more focused tribe and see where it would take us. We've written some papers on sex and social stability and John did a couple of papers that were an overview of the culture and how the antisex movement can take the culture down."

At one point, a vice president at IBM asked them to submit a proposal for building a community that would nurture and create a future generation of creative leaders. But the proposal for Project Synergy was never funded.

Eventually, they moved to the Bay Area and then a ten-acre property in Nevada. As soon as they arrived, a neighbor told them there were some big cats that were about to be killed because no one would take care of them.

"Being as innocent as he was, John stuck his head into this tiger's mouth," Barbara recalled, "and from then on, they became best friends for the next seventeen or eighteen years."

Suddenly, the Williamsons had found their new passion: Instead of building communities for people, they worked on building them for tigers, servals, cougars, lions and other big cats, creating their own sanctuary.

"Much like Sandstone, we were studying bonding with the cats," Barbara said. "It was the most exciting life we could have hoped for in these last seventeen years with the cats."

Before his death, John was working to build what he and Barbara called Tiger Touch University Retreat, which would rescue and care for and house up to 100 exotic cats, and also allow them a safe place to breed and prevent extinction. More information can be found at www.ttur.org.

It wasn't until two weeks before he passed away that John was diagnosed with lung cancer, which quickly spread. He is survived by his wife Barbara and his daughter and granddaughter, who live in Washington and Alaska.

"I was just laughing the other day," Barbara recalls, "because I was remembering just a couple of months ago when John went to the grocery store with me. Within seconds, he was surrounded by women who were laughing and chatting with him. They loved his vibes and loved him as a human being. The only thing he ever promised me is that I'd have an exciting life, and man, he delivered on that big time!"

There were several other tributes to John in different newspapers from all over the United States and worldwide. I must admit to being a little surprised that he had touched so many people, that his views had piqued the curiosity of so many. He was indeed a guru, a charismatic leader in so many ways, a gentle guide to a better way of life. Low-key, laid back, calm, and cool, it took a lot to ruffle his feathers, and even then he was still soft-spoken and tender. I miss him so.

I remember one evening at Sandstone when this very successful gentleman approached me to thank me for an unforgettable weekend. "It was like falling down the rabbit hole from *Alice in Wonderland*," he laughed. "Exciting, crazy, a kaleidoscope of wild emotions, a thrill ride I will always remember." He took my hand and brought it to his lips, kissing it softly. "Thank you, Miss Barbara, for the most magical, unforgettable weekend of my life."

So let that be Sandstone's legacy—a magical Camelot for one brief and shining moment, too exciting and beautiful to ever be forgotten.

And for me? I get to wrap myself in the warm memories of an extraordinary life.

www.ingramcontent.com/pod-product-compliance
Lightning Source LLC
LaVergne TN
LVHW042249070526
838201LV00089B/84